TALES FROM THE DALLAS COWBOYS SIDELINE

TALES FROM THE DALLAS COWBOYS SIDELINE

A COLLECTION OF THE GREATEST COWBOYS STORIES EVER TOLD

CLIFF HARRIS AND
CHARLIE WATERS

FOREWORD BY ROGER STAUBACH

SPORTS PUBLISHING

Sports Publishing books may be purchased in bulk at special discounts for sales promotion, corporate gifts, fund-raising, or educational purposes. Special editions can also be created to specifications. For details, contact the Special Sales Department, Sports Publishing, 307 West 36th Street, 11th Floor, New York, NY 10018 or info@skyhorsepublishing.com.

Sports Publishing® is a registered trademark of Skyhorse Publishing, Inc.®, a Delaware corporation.

www.sportspubbookscom

10 9 8 7 6

Library of Congress Cataloging-in-Publication Data is available on file.

Cover design by Tom Lau
Cover photo courtesy of AP Images

ISBN: 978-1-61321-890-7
e-ISBN: 978-1-61321-912-6

Printed in the United States of America

Our dreams were born when we were kids. We lived those dreams. We dedicate this account to our own kids and pray they will have a chance to live a dream like we did.

We also dedicate it to the memory of Tom Landry in hopes that his life priorities (faith, family and football) will survive the test of time. When asked what he'd like on his tombstone, Landry replied, "At some point in time, I'd like my players to say, 'The coach was right.'"

He was, you know.

Contents

Foreword
By Roger Staubach

It was no coincidence that as soon as Cliff Harris and Charlie Waters joined the Dallas Cowboys in 1970, we competed in five Super Bowls in the next eight years. Charlie and Cliff anchored our secondary as twin safeties during those championship seasons.

Harris and Waters might as well have been actual brothers or even twins. They were so inseparable on and off the field that you almost thought of them as a single entity. Cliff and Charlie could have co-starred in the movie *Butch Cassidy and the Sundance Kid*.

Great players often spring from humble origins. So it was with this rare pair who both ultimately became known for their propensity for big plays in big games. They both made All-Pro and were respected throughout the league for their many Pro Bowl appearances. However, in the beginning, neither was a sure-shot future star.

Harris was a free agent from tiny Ouachita Baptist University in Arkansas. When overlooked in the NFL draft, Cliff ultimately proved them all wrong by becoming one of the best free safeties ever. Waters came as a third-round choice—a quarterback-turned-receiver—at Clemson. Nor was he finished changing positions in the NFL. Charlie started out as a cornerback before he found comfort and stardom at strong safety.

Cliff changed the way free safeties play the position. I think he's Hall of Fame material because of it. He gave us more flexibility on defense because he could play the run.

He made lots of tackles near the line of scrimmage. He was not one-dimensional, like old-school, deep-center safeties. That allowed coach Tom Landry to design our defenses a bit differently because he had run support from Cliff along with pass defense.

Harris showed that safeties didn't have to just hang back to prevent long passes and make interceptions. A safety could mix it up and become an intimidating factor physically along with being a ball hawk. Cliff showed how to do it, which is how he got his nickname of Captain Crash. We knew he'd rather put a big hit on someone than intercept a pass.

I remember Cliff saying, "If you step in front of a receiver and intercept a pass, he'll be a little upset. But if you blast him, turn his helmet around, then he'll be looking for you. A good hit just makes my job easier. After a hit, I ask, 'Was it worth it?'"

Charlie was an Xs and Os student. Charlie should be a coach today because he was like a coach when he played. He understood the game, and not only from strong safety. He knew the other 10 positions on defense. And they were as important to him as his own place in the overall scheme.

"The most important thing," Waters once said, "is not my individual performance, but to make sure everybody plays the right defense."

Waters was like Bob Lilly and Randy White—misplaced in his original position. Lilly flowered after moving from defensive end to tackle, and White moved from linebacker to tackle. Before settling as a gifted strong safety, Charlie knew tough times at cornerback.

He once put the cornerback experience in wry terms by saying: "If you learn by mistakes, I ought to be a genius."

At crunch time, Cliff and Charlie were there and always seemed to make the critical plays. Cliff's calling card was the big hit, while Charlie's became the interception. Waters made 50 career interceptions, including an NFL-record nine during playoffs. He turned many games with a stolen pass, fumble recovery or blocked punt.

Both of these guys were as competitive as I was. Cliff and I used to compete just jogging around the field to get warmed up. We both wanted to win the jog. I knew Cliff was faster, so I'd take off when he wasn't ready and listen to him complain later.

Passing drills were just as competitive. I think that was healthy. It always helped me in practice to throw against people who went full out in the secondary. Cliff and Charlie played the way they practiced—at top speed. They were the best safeties I ever played against. They made me better.

They supported each other on the field, knew exactly where the other would be and how he'd react. They had an uncommon, often unspoken communion that allowed each to adjust instinctively. Cliff and Charlie knew the scheme so well, that they even made up some new coverages during a game.

Their tales share an inside look at the complex personality of the great Tom Landry and offer a unique angle of our (America's) team. It includes stories that have never been told, yarns about teammates and rival players, big games and Super Bowls, and humorous replays of incidents from an era when we were all a lot younger. But none are better than the tale of the twin safeties—Cliff and Charlie.

Acknowledgments

Thanks to our partners at Energy Transfer and especially our families for indulging our commitment to this work. Also, special thanks to Kelcy Warren, Ray Davis, Mike Warren, Clay Kutch, Jennifer Jones, Lovita and Ken Irby, Dick Whittingham, Frank Luksa, *The Dallas Morning News*, the Dallas Cowboys (Rich Dalrymple and Brett Daniels), the *Dallas Cowboys Official Weekly* (Russ, Cheryl, and Sharon), Erin Linden-Levy and Roger Staubach.

Introduction
By Cliff Harris

The Game Today

The wintry holiday season is the crescendo to a fall football season with all the exciting college bowl games and the NFL playoff games taking place. They all seem to be at different tempos than the games played the rest of the year, finally climaxing with the Super Bowl now held in early February.

The game of football is thriving with loaded stadiums, and there are bowl games and playoff games all over the TV, with coverage on 10 or 12 stations. With the recent change to a national college playoff system, there seems to be even more interest in the game. Hopefully the changes to the rules in response to concerns over the prevalence of concussions will enable players to be healthier and the popularity of the game to remain strong.

To me, the NFC and AFC Championship games are the most entertaining games to watch all year. There is a certain intensity that cannot be matched in any other game, including the Super Bowl. During my era we won 5 NFC championship games and I played in 7. I think back about those games and remember how exciting they all were.

The Super Bowl is a game that defines many players' lives. Your play in a Super Bowl is often a reflection of your career. The press is there every day to visit with you about who you are and what you are going to do in the big game. Your predictions, statements, and play are certainly scrutinized and magnified for many years to come.

At this year's Super Bowl many interesting feelings flowed through my body and mind. I thought about how fortunate I was to play for the Dallas Cowboys and to play in five Super Bowls.

The Cliff Harris Award . . . What "IT" Takes

Today, I realize I have been blessed. To be as healthy as I am considering my style of play with the intensity and my reckless nature and lack of fear, I must be. I certainly could have been seriously injured so many times.

I realize that I know more now than I did then about the odds that were stacked against me to even have a chance to get a tryout to play pro football.

Since the previous iteration of our book, the Cliff Harris Award has been created, which allows me and my committee to determine the best defensive player in small colleges across the nation. A trophy is presented to the best defensive small college player of the year in Division II, Division III, and NAIA. There are approximately 500 small colleges in all of these divisions. At the end of every year athletic directors and sports information directors from coast to coast all across the United States from every division send to us their choices regarding their top players. There are generally around 125 nominees. The nominees are incredible players. After hours of poring over the stats we find in our final group, there are many All-Conference and Division Players of the Year, two-year All-Americans, and several times Players of the Week.

The process has become very difficult and there has been much exhausting time spent to fairly determine a winner. Several of my famous former teammates, as well as some of my fierce competitors, now friends from other teams, study all the choices so that we can pick a winner at the end of the season, by Christmas Eve every year.

Going through the qualifications while looking at all these great players makes me realize the talent that is available all over the nation and yet, most of these young men do not even get a chance to try out or even go to a training camp. Bringing recognition to these small colleges and these young men is the main reason that I give the Award. I also find it humorous to think that I did not even have enough honors when I played in college to even be considered to win my own award.

At the packed dedication ceremony dinner the room was full of athletes of all levels receiving awards—high school, college and others aspiring for a chance at pro football. Before giving my Award, I spoke about having "IT," something special that winners have. Is "IT" heart, passion, and intensity? I believe yes, and that there is something else involved in the making of these players that take them to the highest levels of achievement in anything.

In my many years at the Cowboys training camp I'd seen a great number of tremendous athletes competing to make the team. They have great ability, but very few have "IT." I knew during my time with the Cowboys who on my team and which opponents had that special something that made them stand out, "IT."

I told these young athletes how difficult it was to make a pro team and that very few would even have a chance to try out. If they had "IT," they would certainly make the team.

Making the roster of a pro football team does certainly take "IT," but there are also many other factors involved. First, an athlete must have the size, strength, and speed, plus most importantly, durability. Football is a game of tolerating pain and performing at top levels even when you are hurting. There is an old saying in football, "You must know the difference between pain and injury." Many thought there is no such thing as "injury."

Fortunately, I was blessed with a very durable body, and though I made it through most of my years with only relatively minor injuries—broken hand, broken ribs, sprained knee, a few concussions—in my last years I had a worsening neck injury that could have left me permanently paralyzed and actually ended my career. It is as simple as, you must be able to play and perform to make the team.

Another factor is having a spot for you available; either a team has a specific need in a certain position that fits your skill set or that you are good enough to beat out an existing player or that the coaches see a spot for you in the future after some years of development.

A "Thinking" Process

Having a system that fit your characteristics and style was critical. In my case, the Landry "Flex" system was designed perfectly to fit my strengths and nature. One of the options open in the Cowboys' defensive scheme was the free safety position or another possibility was to move an existing player into a new role.

When I came to training camp my rookie year, there was a spot open, free safety. The Cowboys coaches were considering moving Mel Renfro to safety from his stellar play at corner. That is a typical coach's move for players, to go from corner to safety. The Hall of Famer was one of the best athletes that has ever played for the Cowboys. He was a supreme cover corner, though he was not a physical type of player. If they had moved him, he probably would have been an All-Pro safety but, thank goodness for me, he made an even better cornerback.

Tom Landry's "Flex" defense was a very coordinated, well-oiled machine; at every position one had a clearly defined role and quickly moved to a specific spot when the ball was snapped that perfectly meshed with all the other players. There was no weak spot, theoretically. Sometimes we felt that we were all just cogs in the "Flex" wheel, just replaceable parts in a clock. Knowing that we were "cogs" and could be replaced was an insecurity that drove and enhanced our performance.

Tom Landry was a defensive back who played for the New York Giants in the '50s. I believe he saw something of himself in me and that I helped complete the puzzle of his "Flex" coordinated defense. I got it, the "Flex," and understood very well how it worked. I was a player that filled the gaps or holes that were created when a player made a mistake and could not make it to his defined "spot" or play his role after the snap of the ball. Human error or one of our guys getting beaten, was something that did not happen when the defense was drawn up on the chalk board, something the

"Flex" did not account for. Being beaten by an opponent or mistakes where players went the wrong way were not calculated in the synchronized perfect "Flex" system.

I was given an innate ability, maybe a primal instinct, when the ball was snapped and as the blur of a play was developing I could quickly diagnose where it was going and where to go to stop it and then make an impact when I got there. When a linebacker or one of the defensive linemen was cut off and could not make it to his spot, I would be there to fill in the "gap" in his "perfect" system.

The "Flex" fit me in many other ways as well. Disguise was a key component to the Flex's success. From a free safety's standpoint keeping a quarterback guessing as to where you were going and the role you were playing, costing the QB the extra milliseconds trying to figure out what you were doing, meant more time for our very talented defensive linemen and linebackers to get to and sack the QB.

The "Flex" had so many different looks and complicated defenses a QB never really knew where to attack its weakness. When the ball was snapped and I would make a move by running in one direction, this would give the QB an impression that we were in a certain pass defense that maybe looked as if I was helping one cornerback on inside routes, when in fact, my responsibility was on the other side of the field. I would turn, spin around, and help Charlie Waters on a deep route of the tight end. Then, because of the uncertainty of what I was doing, the QB might momentarily freeze, which would give time for Bob Lilly, Lee Roy, Randy

White, or others in our group of talented guys to pull a confused QB down. Of course, having an incredible pass rush and pressure on the QB worked in my favor and allowed me to take these risks.

It was truly a game of "cat and mouse" between me and the QB and the offensive coordinator upstairs in the booth. I could almost hear them saying "dang" or worse. After the QB was trapped after a hesitation, I could hear them saying "wow, just when I thought Cliff was going to the strongside to help Mel, he spun around and helped Charlie on the weakside." . . . It was so much fun.

Around the league, because my competition with the QB was not a physical as much as it was a mental game, anticipating every play was, in fact, more like a chess match between me and the QB. This is one reason that I became friends with many of the QBs around the league. However,

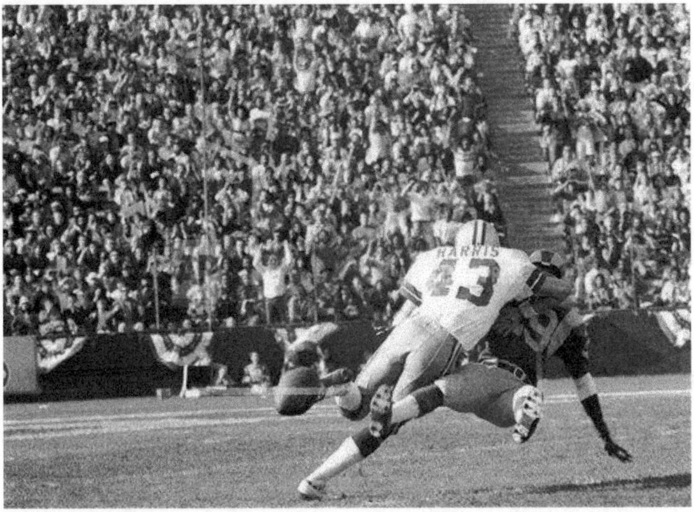

Receivers required a more physical approach. ***AP Photo***

not so with the wide receivers. They required an entirely different mentality . . . it was a more physical approach, so they would be no longer be anxious to venture into my territory.

A Dynamic Duo

Charlie Waters came in my rookie year and replaced me in my spot as free safety while I was fulfilling my military obligation, and later we teamed up, with him playing at corner. Ultimately though, we became a very effective safety duo when he moved over and became an All-Pro strong safety. By us working together in his many different positions made for a perfect scenario when we became safeties. We had much fun and success working up many schemes to confuse opposing QBs.

Another subtle element to performing well was the ability to "take coaching." Many people in life have a hard time taking criticism. For me, I knew that pointing out my mistakes and not making the same mistakes again certainly made me a better player. My performance was a constant improvement process of eliminating mistakes and refining positive skills.

I had a very strong-willed and forceful coach in Gene Stallings. He was not only an unquestionably great teacher and coach but also an honorable man and my mentor, who is a good friend today. We did, however, have a few moments of disagreement, generally about running certain defenses one way or another, the way I wanted to do it and the way he wanted me to do it . . . When he wanted me to move one way in a certain defense and I wanted to move another, or I wanted to run one defense and he wanted another, he would always have a quiet reply—"Go talk to Tom about it." Sometimes when he really wanted us to do something, he would tell Charlie and me, "Now pay attention. It's just a little thang but . . ." He was great fun during those years and even more now today.

The Landry Approach

As for Coach Landry, he would have a much more subtle and less direct, but forceful approach. He wanted to let me know in his own way not to be too aggressive on one of my favorite defenses to run, which was a Flex Weak 34. That specific defensive was designed for me to take away the deep routes on the strong side of a "Brown" formation. Simply, when the ball was snapped, from my position, I would run laterally across the field from the weak side to the strong side of the offensive formation and give support to the inside routes, like the post route, to the strong side corner and at the same time, help the strong safety with any deep routes of the tight end.

This was the type of defense that gave me the latitude to make my movements look like another defense. The goal, therefore, was to confuse the opponent for those few split seconds. That would give our crushing defensive linemen the opportunity to trap the QB or cause him to potentially throw the ball up for grabs.

We would run this defense typically on "Brown," because it primarily was a running formation but had a very challenging play action pass associated with it. The "34" was signaled on the field by holding up one hand with 4 fingers extended. The "Brown" look was where the FB lined up directly behind the QB and the halfback was lined up on the weakside behind the weakside tackle.

We knew, dictated from our computerized printouts, the most often run play from "Brown" was the fullback running "off tackle" to the weak side. That was a play that I loved to come up and make the tackle on. When I would see the play developing I hit it fast and would quickly come up and try to make the tackle on the FB right at the line of scrimmage.

Coach Landry's issue was not my making the tackle on the run but the fake run with a play action, it was the deep pass to the post on the strong side exactly where I was supposed to be covering. The play was called a "Fake" Slant 34, Wing Post. Therefore, if it wasn't the run play I expected and I was faked out I would turn and see a deep pass over my head; where I was supposed to be helping, the corner would most certainly end up a TD pass.

In trying to help me understand the significance of making sure I made the play on the deep pass and minor insignificance of making the tackle at the line of scrimmage, Coach Landry in his subtle and quiet but firm way, told me, "Cliff, you know you have deep responsibility to help the corner on the deep post route when we play Flex Weak 34." He was trying to point out to me that I had to make the post route or I was in trouble if it was a pass and not a run. I knew what he was saying and merely answered, "Yes sir." He was telling me you can be aggressive as you want but . . . don't make a mistake! I got it!

There was always a fine line in my style of play. I took chances based on my ability to quickly analyze the plays. If I had been wrong, as Coach Landry was telling me, I would have been on the bench, not the field. I would not say that I was right every time, but I guess I was right more times than I was wrong.

A Moment to Remember

When I look back on my life and think about my incredible time with the Cowboys, what first comes to my mind is a vision of the very end of Super Bowl XII. I was in the new Superdome in New Orleans in 1978, after the 1977 season. We were beating the Denver Broncos 24-10 in the 4th quarter with only a few minutes left and the clock ticking down.

The atmosphere seemed mystic with the fans all going crazy, and there was a palpable electricity. I remember we were huddled on the field; it was between plays when I took a moment to look around and see the bright field but dimly lit stands of the Superdome. It was filled with screaming, berserk fans dressed in completely contrasting colors, either Cowboys Blue or Orange Crush. Craig Morton, Broncos QB, poked his head up and looked at me before they broke their huddle. As I looked around, suddenly time slowed down, I glanced up, and I saw the clock with the seconds slowly ticking away. At that moment, I thought about my life. This is such a great time! Even with victory in our hands,

I said to myself, I wish we could just play one more quarter. As crazy as that may sound, I truly wanted that to happen. I didn't want the game to end and was enjoying playing and performing under the pressure it created, knowing that this was my seventh year in the league and my time as a Dallas Cowboy was coming to an end. I had lived the timeframe of a whole life yet in only a few years as a professional football player. In ordinary life, I had come in as a fearless young man, a rookie, with no experience, and all I had to rely on was my innate talent and skill. Then, as the years passed and I matured and gained more experience, I began to better figure out the "system" and make it work for me by using more cunning thinking and less energy to win my "strategic" game on the field.

"A Gift"

Such is the way of life. In every occupation, you come in eager and ready to go but inexperienced, wasting time and energy; eventually, you learn from your mistakes and become more savvy, efficient, and effective.

I truly had the chance to live completely another lifetime, and now I am very happy in another phase of still another life not in football. I will be eternally grateful for my now seemingly unreal years in my "lifetime" spent with the Dallas Cowboys and all of the incredible opportunities and wonderful life it has given me in "today's" life.

I do not and will not ever take any of it for granted. My time with the Dallas Cowboys has given me the experience to know how to live and how to manage this second stage of my life. Accepting and knowing how to learn from your mistakes, making the most of your opportunity, and growing is the key to success and happiness. I am not saying that life does not have disappointments; it does, and you just have to fight through them and make the best of any situation and say your prayers.

CHAPTER 1

The Early Years

CLIFF'S TALE Bob Lilly and the Rookie

Bob Lilly was the foundation from which Tom Landry built his famous Doomsday Defense—a "thinking man's" defense. Bob was not only a very talented athlete, but he was also an inspiring leader. When Bob said something in a meeting, everyone listened and really took what he said to heart. He was one of the few who would stand up and vocalize his opinion about our game plan. He was there from the very beginning of the team and was frustrated with the can't-make-it-to-the-big-one criticism. He was the driving force and was very focused on making the Cowboys a championship team.

Lilly was a legend even before I came to the Cowboys. I will never forget the first time I saw him. I don't really know what I expected him to look like, but Bob was not built like a muscleman. He was a redheaded, ruggedly handsome guy with a long barrel chest that was the same size from his neck to his waist. He was fair-skinned and freckled. In training camp, Bob cut squares out of his pants in a checkerboard fashion to keep cool. I don't know if it worked, but it looked pretty funny when he took his pants off and his white legs had red, sunburned checkerboard squares all over them.

One of the most exciting moments of my Cowboy career—I'll never forget it—was finding out I made the team and getting to start my first game at the same time.

After several weeks of a really tough training camp, the time came to make the final cut. There were three defensive safeties who were in the running to make the team: Charlie Waters, Richmond Flowers (an Olympic hurdler from the University of Tennessee) and me. Richmond was a second-year player, which meant he knew the system. Charlie and I relied on Richmond's experience, insight and wisdom anticipating the coaches' next moves. Authoritatively, he told us what was going to happen: They (the coaches) are going to cut one of us, one is going to the taxi squad, and the other has a chance to make the starting lineup. Hearing this from Richmond, I will never forget my anxiety in the meeting when Landry began to announce the team. The room was filled with nervous players wondering about their futures and whether they might be going back home. Landry stood up and began to announce the starting lineup. He named me as the starting free safety for the Dallas Cowboys. I wanted to stand up and yell, but I kept my cool.

My first home game of the 1970 regular season as a Dallas Cowboy was against the New York Giants in the Cotton Bowl. Though I was a starter, I still played on the specialty teams. I went down on the first kickoff and made the tackle. Then I ran off the field. I was standing next

Cliff's roommate, Pat Toomay, steady Larry Cole, and the great Bob Lilly. ***Photo courtesy of Cowboys Weekly***

to Coach Landry on the sidelines looking at the defensive huddle at the 20-yard line. Coach Landry looked over at me and very calmly said, "Cliff, don't you think you need to go in?" I was so excited that I forgot to stay in on defense.

I sprinted onto the field and broke into the huddle just as Lee Roy Jordan was calling the defensive signals. That moment will forever be frozen in my mind. When I took my position in the circle with the Cowboys' defensive stars, I was bent over at the waist with my hands on my knees. I was looking right into Bob Lilly's face. He looked over at me very seriously and said, "Rookie, we're going to the Super Bowl this year, and I don't want you to screw it up. Do you understand?"

"Yes, sir," I said.

We did, in fact, go to the Super Bowl that year, but were beaten by the Baltimore Colts. At the end of the game, Lilly threw his helmet a record 40 yards in disgust, but we were on our way. We had beaten the Cowboy no-Super Bowl curse.

CHARLIE'S TALE Starr Struck

My first preseason game as a pro athlete was against the Green Bay Packers—the same Green Bay Packers that were coached by the legendary Vince Lombardi. We all grew up watching Bart Starr, Paul Hornung, Fuzzy Thurston, Boyd Dowler, Jim Taylor—household names. Because I was a quarterback in college, it was natural for me to idolize Bart Starr, the Packers' Hall of Fame quarterback. I was just 20 years old, and Starr had to be 34 when we played them.

I was sent into the game halfway through the first quarter. Bart Starr was scheduled to play only the first half. When we broke the huddle and I dropped back to my safety position, the rush of excitement overwhelmed me as I realized that I was actually on the field with the greatest quarterback in the NFL. I gathered myself and settled into the job at hand, careful about being blinded by awe.

The first two plays were running plays—the famous Green Bay sweep. We stopped them clean. The two failed

Bart Starr—my hero.
Photo © Vernon J. Biever

runs left Starr's Packers with a third-and-nine situation. He dropped back and looked downfield for an open receiver. Four seconds into the play, Starr was still in the pocket. He raised the ball to throw, but changed his mind and tucked it under his arm, simultaneously stepping up. After two steps, the pocket was closing and nobody was open, so Bart Starr elected to make a rare scramble in an attempt to gain the first down.

When he crossed the line of scrimmage he started veering toward the sideline. I closed in on him, hemming him in.

He and I both saw the first-down marker, so the collision occurred about two yards short of the stick. He was lunging for that marker, and I was exploding to keep him from it. We collided, and I drove him toward the row of photographers bordering the playing field. We slid a good four to five yards on the slick artificial turf, with me on top of him.

When we came to a halt, we were facing each other, helmet to helmet, and Bart said, "Nice hit!"

The kid inside me took over and I replied, "Thanks! Could I have your autograph?"

He chuckled and answered, "Maybe after the game."

Signing Bonus

The management of the Dallas Cowboys, and in particular Gil Brandt, vice-president of personnel development, did some things that looked pretty bizarre to their competition, such as drafting a quarterback when he was locked into a four-year wartime commission as a naval officer. When you do such things and they don't work out, people think you're crazy or stupid. But if they do work, you're a visionary—you're thinking outside the box. The success that the Cowboys had with the likes of Roger Staubach speaks for itself. I don't know if we can classify Gil Brandt as a visionary or not, but I do know he was a good negotiator who flirted with being just a little slimy.

The Cowboy players had a saying: "Gil Brandt knew we loved the game so much that we would play for nothing… so that's what he paid us, nothing." After I was drafted in the third round out of Clemson, it was Gil's job to try to sign me. Only the first-round picks used agents, so he was dealing directly with me. The entire package Brandt offered amounted to $12,000—not bad money for those days.

Brandt was a smooth operator, at least compared to kids 20 years his junior—the ones he was negotiating with. His smoothness bordered on slick. But make no mistake; he was really good at what he did. He hailed from the Big D, a high-profile city, considered to be a "happening place."

When Gil Brandt showed up at my fraternity house on the Clemson campus, which is nestled in the foothills of the Blue Ridge Mountains, he was dressed in a beautiful Armani suit and sported a great pair of alligator tassel shoes. Impressed, I felt compelled to compliment him on his dress, especially those awesome alligator shoes.

We didn't come to terms that day, and he left South Carolina to return to Texas. Understandably, I was a little down.

Innovative player personnel guru Gil Brandt.
Photo courtesy of the Dallas Cowboys

Four days later I received a box in the mail from Texas. I opened it, and to my delight, there was a pair of those alligator shoes, just like Gil's—perfect and just my size. I thought, "Wow, I'm in the big time now!" I had never had or even seen anything as nice as those shoes. They were more beautiful than I had remembered. What a nice gesture on Gil's part.

Three months passed and we still hadn't settled on contract terms. Our reporting date was closing in when Gil finally offered me an additional $3,000 signing bonus to bring the total package to $15,000. We agreed over the phone and he followed up by overnighting my contract to me at school. I executed it and sent it back the same day.

Four days later I received my signing bonus check. Also enclosed with the check was an invoice for those alligator shoes; their cost had been deducted from my bonus check.

Welcome to the business of "professional" football.

CLIFF'S TALE *Jaw Breaker*

When I signed a free agent contract with the Cowboys, I had no idea what to expect in terms of competition to make the team. My college football career was played at a small college that my father attended, Ouachita Baptist University in Arkadelphia, Arkansas, in the NAIA. The players trying out for the Cowboys were made up of the best players—college stars from all over the U.S. from the large Division I universities down to small colleges the size of Ouachita. There were 120 rookies who had signed free agent contracts or were drafted by the Cowboys that year. The rookies who made it would ultimately play on the Cowboys' first Super Bowl team against the Baltimore Colts in Super Bowl V.

In the draft, the Cowboys felt they needed to shore up some weaknesses in the secondary. I was scrapping for a defensive back job along with 20 other top-notch athletes. Some were draft picks, but most were free agents. The Cowboys had drafted five DBs from their 19 picks: an All-America free safety from Texas Tech named Denton Fox, Charlie Waters from Clemson, Mark Washington, a great corner from Morgan State, Seaburn Hill from Arizona State, and Pete Athas from the Canadian league.

The free safety spot needed to be filled because the Cowboys were considering moving Mel Renfro from safety to corner. He was better suited for the corner position with his excellent speed and coverage ability. Mel was a master cover man, but was not known as a hitter. For that reason, the Cowboys had a weakness and were vulnerable in the middle on "slant" routes.

The "in" route consistently gained yardage, because the Flex defense did not allow the linebackers to easily drop back from their run support positions and cover the short middle pass. It was also not Mel's style to bust 'em when they came inside.

I loved the slant route from a free safety position, because I could unload on a receiver just as he touched the ball. I attacked where Mel would cover. Thank goodness for the difference, or there may not have been an opening for me. When a receiver ran an inside route on me, he knew what to expect...a helmet under his chin!

In training camp I was trying hard and hitting everybody—all the time. I didn't care who they were or when it happened, I didn't think I would be around very long anyway. I wanted to try to make an impression, though. And I wanted to make the team!

Pete Athas was one of those very talented guys trying to make the team. He was older and had played Canadian league ball for a couple of years and knew the "ropes." Anyone who had been in the league for more than one year was revered by all of us rooks. Pete was a savvy guy who ran a 4.5 40 and could cover. I considered him my main competition for free safety.

To help make comparisons between players, during practice and games the Cowboys kept every statistic you could imagine—how many passes the QBs completed and for how long; how many passes the receivers caught; and, more importantly to me, how many passes were caught against which DBs. One day in practice, one of the drills was man-to-man coverage. It did not matter, rookie or veteran, all the DBs had to cover all the receivers. There were also about 20 receivers trying to fill six or seven spots. The line of receivers formed opposite the line of DBs, and we covered whoever matched up with us.

It was a hot afternoon in the desert of Thousand Oaks, and everyone was on edge. My turn came up, and I was matched against Reggie Rucker. Rucker was a veteran of about four years—from my perspective, an old-timer. He was also a tough guy. I lined up on him, poised to cover his route. He blasted off and made an outside move to the sideline and then broke for the deep middle. He was running a post route to the middle of the field. I bit just enough on his outside fake for him to get a step on me. Roger was the QB, and he launched a perfect spiral towards Reggie's outstretched hands. Just as the ball was coming down into his hands, I reached out very discreetly and grabbed the back of Reggie's jersey. He dove, but the ball floated just past his outstretched hands. My gentle tug had held him back and slowed him just enough.

When he missed the pass, he got really pissed! He jumped up and said that I held him. Then he tried to punch me. We wrestled around for a bit and that was it…I thought. The coaches made a note of his no-catch and my breakup.

Then Pete Athas made a career-changing mistake. After practice in the locker room as they were walking to the showers, Pete told Margene Adkins, a rookie wide receiver, "If Cliff had been a black guy, Reggie would not have fought with him." Margene scrambled over to the vets' locker room, found Reggie and told him what Pete had said. Reggie really blew his top, I assume because of the racial nature of the comment. He came over to the rookie locker room and found Pete, who had just finished his shower and was sitting on a bench with a towel around his waist. Reggie stood in front of Pete and said, "If you have something to say to me, say it to my face!" Then he smashed Pete right in the jaw. The impact broke Pete's jaw and sent him to the hospital for a couple of weeks. Ultimately he was cut from the Cowboys, but he was with the New York Giants for a few years.

I haven't seen Pete since that time, but I had a chance to thank Reggie a few years ago for helping me make the team when I was a rookie.

Wake Up… It's Just a Dream!

The U.S. was a mixed-up place, full of turmoil, when I was in college in the late '60s and early '70s. People, especially college students, all over the U.S. were rebelling against authority, and the Vietnam War was the main reason. Some were burning American flags and protesting the war, at times peacefully and at others violently—some were even shot for it at Kent State. People were moving to Canada and other countries to avoid the draft.

The army draft system worked like this: all the days of the year were thrown into a big hopper; they were mixed up, then randomly pulled out and assigned a number in the order they were pulled. My birthday, November 12, was draft number 66. Any guys with numbers under 166 were drafted and were required to join some branch of the armed services and possibly to go to war. The only alternatives to the draft were college, physical disability deferment, or a quick move out of the country.

The Cowboys had another system. The guys they drafted in the NFL draft were given their army induction physicals in Dallas. Then they would somehow flunk their physical with bad knees or some other ailment. Their potential new players ended with a 4F status, which meant they were unqualified to perform their army duties…but they could play pro football.

I was not drafted by the Cowboys; I was a free agent. Therefore I had to take my physical in Little Rock, Arkansas, and I passed. I called the Cowboys and asked them what to do about my military draft situation. They told me a good way to fulfill my obligation was to join a National Guard unit. I was not given the option of visiting a Cowboys doctor in Dallas for a second opinion.

Fortunately (or not) for me, Ouachita Baptist's team doctor was an orthopedic surgeon from Arkadelphia. By chance, he also headed up an Army Reserve unit and he told me I could join. It was Army Reserve in Little Rock, not National Guard, but I didn't care and joined. It meant I had to attend monthly meetings with the unit, but it would not obliterate my season. I went to one meeting and then went off to California to try out for the Dallas Cowboys. The war and the army were way in the back of my mind. Unbelievably, I made the team and, even more unbelievably, the starting lineup.

I was living a dream, busting guys on Sundays in the NFL and having a great year playing free safety for the Dallas Cowboys. The season and all that I had accomplished were about to be in jeopardy. After my second game, about the middle of September, I received some bad news in the mail. The letter stated my reserve unit in Little Rock had been called to active duty, and if nothing changed I was to report to Fort Polk, Louisiana, for basic training at the end of the month.

When I got the letter my heart stopped. I had to reread it. Then I took it to the Cowboy front office and asked, "What can I do?" I did not fully understand what it meant at first. "Do I have to leave the team?"

I was told, "Yes. If nothing changes."

I thought, "How could this happen? During my early years, my coaches told me to quit, but I hung in there anyway. Then, after going to tiny Ouachita Baptist College, I made the starting lineup for the Dallas Cowboys! This is not fair!"

In my first games, I had really performed very well. I had been named MVP for Dallas in two of the first five games. It was the only time that had ever happened to a rookie. I was now devastated by the thought that it was all coming to an end. The Cowboys' front office got very busy then, trying to find a way to at least delay my training until after the season or move me to another unit. Closing the barn door a little late, I thought.

The enterprising Gil Brandt, director of player personnel for the Cowboys, started working through all the powerful Cowboy connections to see if I might have any other options. He reasoned: What difference would it make to the army whether I went to training in September or January, after the season?

Gil took immediate and drastic action. He flew down to the 4th Army headquarters in San Antonio the next week to speak to the person in charge of the timing of my active duty. Gil's proposal was to delay the starting time. The training was nine weeks long, so I could play the whole season and then go to the training. Gil's task was to find someone who could make that happen.

When Gil reached the highly secured guard gate, he told them he was with the Dallas Cowboys and that he needed to get through because he had an urgent meeting with the general. They pointed him toward his office. Gil found out that the general had gone to relax in a steam bath at the spa on the base. Gil took off for the spa. He worked his magic and got in. He disrobed, put on a towel and headed into the steam bath. Through all the steam, Gil managed to find the general, covered with towels. Gil told him who he was and what he wanted. The general couldn't believe he got in, but essentially told him that he could not let me off. That didn't stop Gil.

I found out later that Gil went all the way to Melvin Laird, the secretary of defense, to plead my case. The answer was still that they could not make an exception for a pro football player and that I had to go.

While the Cowboys were working on my case, I was busy. I played a couple more games in Dallas and was really getting into the groove. The last game I was to play, unless something was worked out, would be in Minnesota.

The Saturday before our game with the Vikings, we were on the field at Metropolitan Stadium in Minneapolis doing our typical Saturday walk-through when Gil Brandt walked over to me. He said they had not been able to work it out and that I had to report Monday morning to basic training. I will never forget how I felt when I heard that news. My head began to spin—talk about losing my focus!

That Sunday, as the game began, I remember thinking, "This could be my last pro game!" During the game, our whole team was not performing very well. We were getting our tails kicked by the Vikes. Right before half, I was told to take a dive—pretend I was hurt. Then I would have a reason not to go to Fort Polk.

I didn't do it, and after a real whipping, we flew back to Dallas. I got home at about one in the morning. It was a short night! Early that next morning I was in a state of shock when I left my new Dallas home before the sun rose to catch the flight to my new destiny. I had a 7 a.m. flight out of Love Field and was on my way to Fort Polk, Louisiana, and army basic training.

I was numb when I arrived at the little airport in Leesville, Louisiana. It was full of young men wandering around, not sure where to go. Drill sergeants greeted us and drove us to the base by bus. Most of the other recruits were still teenagers. I was 21, turning 22 in November.

We were delivered to a barracks building to wait for the next stage in the process. There were about 30 wide-eyed guys waiting, like me, to see what would happen next.

A whistle blew and they marched us upstairs to the second floor, which was empty except for a bunch of cots lined up against the wall. They gave us brooms and told us to clean up the room. I didn't take a broom and just went over and sat on one of the cots. I am not a rebellious guy normally, but I was watching my dream vanish before my eyes and wasn't feeling too agreeable. One of the sergeants told me to start cleaning. I replied, "Go to hell!"

He left and a moment later, a lieutenant came in and walked over to the cot where I was perched, not moving for anyone. He leaned over to me and said, "I know who you are and what your problem is, but if you don't get up and start cleaning I'm going to pull out my .45, arrest you, and put you in the brig. You'll serve six months' bad time and will have to start this process all over again. Do you understand?"

I said, "Where's the broom?"

I approach life by trying to make the most of my situation. I had no other option but to be there, so I got into it. I was made platoon leader and was in charge of about 75 lost souls. Amazingly, Gil negotiated a deal with the general that allowed me to fly home on weekends and play in the games, which I did for the rest of the season. I got up early on Saturdays and caught a Southwest Airlines flight into Dallas. I changed uniforms from my army greens to shoulder pads and helmets. Since I was still an inexperienced rookie,

I was primarily returning kicks. My buddy Charlie Waters replaced me at free safety while I was gone and did a very good job.

It was a very difficult experience for me that I will never forget. The next year, I got my job back, and we went to the Super Bowl and won. It just goes to show that when things get tough, always hang in there, because something good will come of it!

CHARLIE'S TALE *Safe and Out*

Gil Brandt could make a deal, and he could think outside the box. The Cowboys gambled on Roger Staubach, and Brandt was instrumental in many of the organization's other bold moves. "Projecting" was the clinical term for gambling on converting players to different positions. The team would patiently wait for the player to achieve the learning curve, and then the Cowboys would benefit from the gamble. For example, the Cowboys took an accomplished running back from college, Mel Renfro, and converted him to a Hall of Fame defensive back. They moved an agile tight end, Rayfield Wright, to the offensive tackle position, and he became All-Pro. They switched quarterback Dan Reeves to running back for more flexibility at that position, and he is the NFL record holder for most touchdowns in one season.

Most projections worked, some didn't. Signing Richmond Flowers in 1969 was a projection that didn't work. Flowers, at six feet, two inches and 190 pounds, had played a little football as a wide receiver for the University of

Richmond Flowers was built for flying over Olympic hurdles, not for head-on collisions. ***Photo courtesy of Cowboys Weekly***

Tennessee, but he had not distinguished himself there. He was much better known as an Olympic medalist in the 110-meter intermediate hurdles. He was fast and graceful, in a strange Richmond kind of way. But he didn't earn any style points when he competed. There was something in the way he moved that reminded you of that scarecrow in *The Wizard of Oz*. Not an image you get from many world-class athletes. Some of his teammates started calling him "Whirlybird," because of the way he flailed his arms when he ran. Maybe all that motion gave him extra lift when he was negotiating the high hurdles. But make no mistake, Flowers was an excellent athlete and he was fast. He was the fastest white guy I had ever seen. Because he was so light on his feet, we said he had hollow bones.

In the summer of 1970, Gil Brandt was batting a thousand (three for three) in the visionary category as all three gambles were paying off. Cliff Harris, Richmond Flowers, and I all made the roster as defensive backs. Cliff, a relatively unknown free safety from Ouachita Baptist, ended up being Brandt's brightest star, becoming the starting free safety at the beginning of the season. Richmond, with his speed, was Cliff's backup free safety, and I was behind Cornell Green at the strong safety position. We were all very active on special teams.

October 25, 1970, was the sixth game of the regular season—Dallas Cowboys versus the Kansas City Chiefs in Kansas City. Cliff Harris was already a star. He had started the first five games after not being drafted, one of those Cinderella stories that make sports so much more fascinating. Cliff had earned national attention when he intercepted a pass in a game against the New York Giants, returning it far enough to set up the go-ahead touchdown before a national television audience. But in mid-September of 1970, President Richard Nixon announced that he was ordering an escalation of the Vietnam War, in what was to become known as the Tet Offensive. Cliff was in the National Guard, and his service obligation was a serious matter. His unit was immediately placed on active duty. On October 25, game day, Cliff was on maneuvers near Leesville, Louisiana, brokenhearted and maybe a little nervous.

Richmond Flowers got the call to replace Cliff. Richmond was elated of course, but like Cliff, probably nervous.

The Kansas City game see-sawed back and forth, and halfway through the third quarter, it was still up for grabs. The Chiefs had the ball. On second and four, Ed Podolak took a hand-off from Len Dawson. Podolak followed a block, broke a tackle, and slipped to the outside. Suddenly there was nothing between him and the Cowboy goal line except yards of grass and white stripes.

But the speedy Richmond Flowers was closing in fast and had the angle on the less-than-speedy Podolak. The sideline hemmed Podolak in. The Whirlybird, now more resembling an attack helicopter, had acquired the target, and he was locked on and closing. Apocalypse now. Smells like victory. Eight or ten yards before impact, it was looking like a kill shot, and it was going to happen right in front of our bench. Tom Landry was standing right there, with his arms crossed. In the emotion of the moment, Landry had even leaned forward a little. Ed Podolak had made good yardage, but he was about to pay the price.

Looking back at what happened next, it might make a better story if Richmond Flowers had been a college baseball player instead of a track star. Richmond had the angle, he had the speed and the size, and he had the timing to make a "statement" tackle on Podolak. This should have been a crunching, mauling, send-for-the-jaws-of-life kind of tackle that you see on the NFL highlights.

The only thing is, Richmond didn't tackle Ed.

You see, Richmond, when he was about five yards away, didn't explode into Podolak with his head and shoulders the way we football players are trained to do. Instead, he launched himself into Podolak feet first, and with a perfect hook slide, he skillfully entangled Ed Podolak's feet and legs. Ed eventually stumbled down like one of those walking *Star Wars* machines did when the good guys did a cable wrap on their ankles.

What Richmond did, you could say, resembled a trip. It wasn't really, though. Rather, it was more of an entanglement—the result of a beautiful slide, one that was quite graceful.

There were so many flags flying it resembled graduation day at the Naval Academy, when all the graduates launch their hats. The head referee, the field judge, and the side judge all saw it as a trip, which, of course, is illegal in football—rare, but illegal.

And it all happened right in front of Tom Landry, who never uncrossed his arms. All the unemotional Landry did was shake his head slowly in disbelief and roll his eyes skyward.

You couldn't tell whether he was praying or promising. We will never know.

This incredible scene was capped when Walt Garrison, who was standing next to Coach Landry, bent his knees in a perfect umpire improvisation, spread his arms out in a sweeping motion and yelled, "He's safe!"

That was the last game Richmond started.

CLIFF'S TALE *Coach Gene Stallings*

At the end of my first year, the Cowboys had accomplished a major goal that had eluded them for years: They made it to the Super Bowl. But they lost, so at the start of training camp the next year they made a few changes. They replaced Bobby Franklin as the secondary coach. Bobby was an intense guy, but he wasn't too much older than the players he was teaching. With strong personalities like Mel Renfro, Cornell Green, and Herb Adderly in the backfield, they needed an equally strong personality to teach the "old dogs" new tricks. Those veterans believed that there wasn't a whole lot a coach could teach them, but we found out there was. Though Bobby was a good coach, he was too close to the guys, and they ran the ship. They had all been All-Pro, and both Mel and Herb are in the NFL Hall of Fame today. Landry wanted to change their attitudes, and he thought a new guy in camp who could stand up to them would accomplish that.

Gene Stallings was hired as the secondary coach, and he was about to be challenged like never before. I will never forget our first practice the afternoon that Gene took the reins. You could tell right away that he was a no-BS guy. The first thing he did was to call us together and tell us about himself and what he expected from us. He started by unloading on us and said, "I am here because I got my ass fired as the head coach of Texas A&M. I won the national championship one year and the next year they fired me! So I am not in a good mood!"

We all thought, "Oh, boy! Are we in for it!"

The young guys, like me, Charlie Waters, and Mark Washington, were still trying to prove ourselves, so we had a different perspective from the All-Pro vets. To get things

Coach Stallings was focused, patient, tough, smart, demanding and calculating.
Photo courtesy of the Dallas Cowboys

going, Gene said, in his drawl, "First thang, I want to hear some enthusiasm from you guys." Of course, Charlie, Mark, and I were enthusiastic and started yelling and screaming. Mel and the older guys looked at each other and said, "False chatter, false chatter." We just chuckled under our breaths.

He then said, "Now we are goin' to do some hittin'!" That is where the All-Pros drew the line. Mel slowly walked over to Gene and said in a very calm voice, "Gene, we don't hit." Gene answered, "We will see about that!"

We proceeded to run through the tackle drills. Charlie, Mark, and I were busting our tails, and Mel's vets didn't even get dusty. We didn't hit either after that. Gene was beginning to learn the system.

We all found that Gene was an excellent coach and teacher. The vets did find out that there was a "thang" or two they could learn from him. He was a classy guy with a Southern drawl that hid his ferocious intensity. He really knew football and how to coach it. He kept most controversies simple—"My way or no way!" Gene liked things to be black and white—no in-betweens. Charlie and I had to learn diplomacy to get what we wanted.

After his tour with the Cowboys, he went on to coach the Arizona Cardinals and from there went to the University of Alabama and won another NCAA national championship. He was responsible for developing my talent and ability to an All-Pro level. Charlie, too, gives credit to Gene for his success. We will always be indebted to him.

There were times, though, that Gene and I did not completely agree about some part of the game plan. Usually we found some happy medium where we both gave a little.

Of course, I generally gave more than Gene, but at least we were making progress.

We were, however, on the same page when it came to preparation. Gene expected the players to become as knowledgeable about our defenses and our upcoming opponents as the coaches were. He demanded that we study. He gave us verbal and written tests all the time. Charlie, Mark, and I really believed in the system and studied diligently. It definitely was advantageous for us to understand the Flex defense and how we could maximize it.

The Landry system really worked for us. The coaches made computer reports, films, breakdowns—everything you could imagine about the team you were about to play—available to us. We knew exactly what to expect on every play—formation, down and distance, the time of the game, the hash mark, all the routes of all the receivers. We were prepared!

Like in other aspects of life, though, the next logical progression from knowledge is opinion. When I did not agree with a particular defense in the game plan or the way we were doing things, I spoke to Gene and told him what I thought and why. He sometimes would tell me, with his deep southern twang, "It's not my job to run the train. I can't even ring the bell! But if that train should jump the tracks, see who catches hell!" I would laugh because I knew what he was telling me: It was out of his hands, and if I had a question I needed to see Coach Landry. I also knew that he might have had the same opinion that I did, but that he couldn't change Landry's plan.

I sometimes did go see Coach Landry, but at least I knew Gene and I were in the same boat—or train.

CLIFF'S TALE

Life in the Fast Lane

Looking back on my years in pro football, I realize that I was very fortunate to have played on such an incredible team as the Dallas Cowboys during such a successful era. There were many great players who not only never made it to the Super Bowl, but never even reached the playoffs. My timing was good. I played with some of football's legends and was led by one of the NFL's all-time best coaches in Tom Landry. His character and influence still shape my life today.

I have always wondered what drives a person to play pro football. Do we risk life and limb for fame and reward? For me it may have been the invincibility of youth and a passion for the game. For playing 10 years in the NFL, I came out very healthy…especially the way I played. I approached the game with 100 percent commitment and reckless abandon, with absolutely no fear. I think it was a combination of my youth and personality at that time.

Today when I see tapes of some of the things I did, I wonder how I survived without serious injury. When I made tackles, I wholeheartedly committed to the impact. I put everything I had into every hit, every time. I think that is how I came out with my health intact. Anyone who plays in the NFL, though, pays a price with his body—some more than others. I was one of the lucky ones.

In our early years we were expected to pay our dues and spend some time on the special teams, better known as the "suicide squads." Generally if you were a starter, you were allowed to focus all of your energy on your position, and you missed most of the special-team action. I was not so fortunate.

Cliff's kickoff returns were like downhill skiing...fast, straight and fearless. ***Photo courtesy of the Dallas Cowboys***

Even though I was a starter, I also played on every special team. As soon as the game started, I would sprint down on kickoffs, then play defense. When we would punt, I played the end position. I would battle blockers all the way to the return man, make the tackle, and then go right into the defensive huddle and play defense. After we stopped our opponents, our defensive guys would trot off to the sidelines to rest and recover. But not me! I headed back in to return the punt. Most of those years, Charlie was back there returning punts with me.

Cliff soon learned that kickoff returns were also dangerous.
Photo courtesy of the Dallas Cowboys

With youth must come a tremendous amount of energy! At the time, I did not complain. I actually enjoyed staying on the field and being involved in as much action as possible.

One of the other positions that I also really enjoyed was playing linebacker on goal-line defense. I lined up next to Lee Roy Jordan, the Cowboys' great middle linebacker, who should be in the NFL Hall of Fame today.

Lee Roy was a very smart and intense guy—a perfect leader for the Landry Flex system. He could also "knock your jock off!" When playing for Bear Bryant at the University of Alabama, Lee Roy was considered the best linebacker in college football. I felt honored to line up next to him and really enjoyed teaming up with him on tackles. Lee Roy took me under his wing early and was a major part of my making the team in the first place.

I thought that one of the most exciting, but dangerous parts of the game was running back kickoffs. I took off and flew when I returned kicks. I had to rely totally on my instincts and reactions. For two years I enjoyed speeding down the field at full throttle, weaving in and out and dodging tacklers from all directions until someone would blindside me. I always tried to get a running start and catch the kickoff moving forward at full speed. I used the same approach in kickoff returns that I did in tackling—100 percent, all out. I would run as fast as I could upfield and go as far as I could go.

To reduce the impact of a tackle, I always tried to hit them first and make them absorb the majority of the force. That was good in theory, but it did not always work. A time or two, I had my bell rung. Only strong ammonia capsules under my nose could bring me back to my senses when that happened.

I compare returning kicks to the thrill a surfer has screaming down a 50-foot wave, a downhill skier gets racing down the mountainside at 90 mph, or someone like my dad, a fighter pilot, in a dogfight. It may have just been in my genes. My dad, O.J. Harris, flew a P-38 fighter plane in WWII in the air force. He was stationed in the South Pacific, where he fought the Japanese. He was once shot down in an attack and paddled on a life raft for two days to the only

American-occupied island in the South China Sea. He must have felt that same excitement dodging the enemy Zeroes' bullets as I felt dodging tacklers.

Early in my career I felt "bulletproof" when I was retuning kickoffs. It was great fun. But I know that if I had ever gone less than 100 percent or hesitated at all, I would have been very vulnerable. Luckily, I came to my senses and got off the kickoff return team without sustaining any long-term damage.

I remember the exact return that changed my enthusiasm for that position. It was a kickoff by the Oakland Raiders, and I was hauling it upfield on the very edge of control. I hurdled one would-be tackler, and just as I came back to earth, Jack Tatum (the killer free safety with the Raiders) was waiting for me like a sledgehammer. The instant my foot hit the turf, he unloaded like a cannon, and his helmet exploded in the middle of my chest and up into my chin. That was the last thing I remembered.

Jerry Tubbs, our linebacker coach and a former Cowboy linebacker great, gave me some practical advice: "Cliff, if you want to play long in the NFL, you can't take those kind of hits. You need to take better care of yourself and not make yourself so vulnerable. Don't return kickoffs."

I took Tatum's motivation and Tubbs's advice and ended my thrilling kickoff-return career.

CLIFF'S TALE *No Respect*

The Dallas equipment room was packed full of the newest and best armor available in the war of football.

The general in charge was a guy by the name of Jack Eskridge. Preparation for practice or game day started in the equipment room. Every day, the first things we picked up from Jack were our "socks and jocks." Then we went to our lockers, where everything else was stored, and geared up.

Jack showed favoritism to veterans, but I think he did not really like anyone. He had a particular dislike for rookies. My first year I wanted to exchange a pair of socks that had holes in the heels and took them up to Jack inside his cage. He said, "You can wear the ones with holes, rookie! I am just like the press, you can't get back at me." Then he threw the socks at me.

The Cowboys always had talented people throughout the organization. Jack might have been a good organizer, but he did not seem to be a very happy person. He was replaced a couple of years later by a talented and friendly guy, Buck Buchanan. Buck could not do enough for you. He was retired from the U.S. Air Force, where he had learned his organizational skills. Everything in the equipment room was always "spit-shined," in pristine shape and in the right compartment. Buck is retired now, but his son Bucky works in the equipment room for the Cowboys today.

People have asked me how I decided to wear number 43. The truth is, I did not decide on that number...I really had no choice. Jack Eskridge assigned me that number. Period. As a rookie, I had very little control over what happened to me. The vets got all the good perks.

Before our first preseason game against the San Diego Chargers, we, the 100 or so rooks and vets who made it through the first barrage of cuts, were given jerseys for the upcoming game. Being assigned a number for the Dallas Cowboys meant you were one step closer to making the team. The rookie games were one thing, but preseason was the real thing.

Unfortunately, as it turned out, Eskridge, who did not like rooks, was the one assigning the jerseys. Remember, "You can't get back at me!"

When I went up to the opening in the cage where Jack practically lived and asked for a game jersey, he threw me number 43. I thought it was a good number, but I knew it had been worn years before by one of the original great Cowboys, Don Perkins. He was an excellent running back who is in the "Ring of Honor" in Texas Stadium.

I told Jack, "This was Perkins's number. I want another number."

He just laughed and said, "Hell, boy, it doesn't really matter. Ouachita, you ain't makin' the team anyway!"

Jack Eskridge also controlled who got what shoes. Having the right equipment is critical to good play. Great-fitting and -feeling shoes are especially important in the skill positions to boost confidence and performance. Today there are multiple brands, styles and colors for all types of sports, but throughout my years in school we did not have any choice. The schools made the choice and we wore what we were given. Similarly, the only choice Eskridge gave us was between shoes made by Wilson or Riddell. Wilson had a black, low-cut, red-bottomed, rubber-cleated, AstroTurf shoe, and Riddell built the standard for the market, the XPs—shoes for grass with black leather uppers and a white band around the top that was attached to the laces so you could tighten the shoes around your ankle.

The XPs were not too heavy, but were durable shoes with steel-tipped nylon cleats for good traction. There were different-sized cleats for different conditions—mud, short grass, high, thick grass. XPs were top of the line at the time in football shoes. I had a lot of confidence in my XPs.

The problem was that AstroTurf came out in 1966 and by my first year in '70, many of the stadiums across the country were using it. With their steel cleats, the XPs did not work on artificial turf. The Wilson AstroTurf shoes were our option, and they were heavy and not designed for speed or cutting hard. I did not like them, but had no other choice.

An undercurrent was developing in Europe. Adidas and Puma, who had been designing and making soccer shoes for many years, decided to approach the American football market. Their shoes were excellent—the forerunners of today's sleek, lightweight shoes. They ultimately took over the football shoe market, but first they had to meet some challenges.

With Jack Eskridge in control, the cool Adidas and Puma shoes never made it to the Cowboys' equipment room. The players' choice continued to be either Ridell or Wilson. The soccer companies were determined to break in, though. The soccer shoe reps got to know a few of our players and some of those sleek shoes began to show up in practice and even in games. Some of the new shoes were white, too, not the traditional black. A revolution was taking place.

Paying players, other than the QBs, to wear apparel started in our first Super Bowl appearance. Some of the players, including me, were paid $500 and some were given 15-inch color TVs to wear either Adidas or Puma. Both Adidas and Puma paid my roommate, Pat Toomay. He wore a pair of Adidas shoes in the first half and a pair of Pumas in the second half of the Super Bowl.

Pat was breaking the mold. His looks belied his actions. A businessman at heart, tall and long-haired Toomay looked like a hippie. He was a really bright guy and a Vanderbilt grad. He was the new breed of player, ahead of his time. His then-radical approach to football was more aligned with present players: Make as much money as you can and play for the team that pays you the most. That was the story of his career path in football.

But the real story was this: Jack Eskridge was losing control.

After the Super Bowl, the soccer companies gave us bunches of shoes—a smart move. It meant great exposure for them and better shoes for us.

Jack, though, was trying to get the players to *buy* the shoes that Adidas and Puma were delivering to the back doors of the equipment room. The players revolted, and the equipment guy, whom we couldn't "get back at," was replaced. Shoeboxes began to fill up our lockers. Charlie and I were in heaven. We had lockers full of new, white soccer shoes—sleek and fast.

But a new controversy was arising about the shoes and also the way players are perceived: old shoes versus new and old players versus young. Which shoes would we choose to wear as a team?

CLIFF'S TALE

"The Times, They Are A-Changin'"

From the beginning of pro football in the 1920s, the players had very few options in football shoes. Looking back at all the old films or videos of the early years of the game, the players all wore heavy, black, high-top, steel-cleated shoes. With the introduction of soccer shoes from Europe came lightweight, white shoes with rubber cleats. One receiver for the Houston Oilers was even nicknamed named Billy "White Shoes" Johnson. At one time, it was a big deal to wear white shoes.

In the old days of football it was more of a team game. The players were tough and macho. There were no face masks! Guys who were considered stars were humble and spoke more of "the team" than themselves. Everything was done in self-sacrifice and "for the team." Guys who tried to stand out were labeled "show boats" or "hot dogs." Those individualists were targets for the opposition. The New York Jets' flamboyant QB Joe Namath was a prime example. Times sure have changed!

After our old equipment guy, who controlled the flow of shoes to the players, was replaced, new high-tech soccer shoes began to appear with more regularity in games. Those shoes were the prototypes of today's football shoes. Most of them were low-cut and white. Most had rubber cleats. Generally, the older guys did not like the white shoes. To them it symbolized individualism over team. The sprinkling of white shoes on the Cowboys' team started to take place in the early '70s in the preseason games following our first Super Bowl. The Cowboys had high visibility around the U.S., so the new shoe guys on the block wanted the Cowboys in their shoes.

During those preseason games, half the guys would wear the new, cool, white soccer shoes they had been given (mainly the young guys) and the other guys would wear the traditional black ones. Coach Landry did not like the non-uniformity. The "serious" part of our year was drawing close. Before one of our last preseason games, Landry, in our first team meeting of the day, addressed the issue of shoes. He suggested that we should act as a team, dress as a team, show conformity and all wear the same uniform, including our shoes. He told us that he was going to step out of the room and let us vote on the shoes we wanted to wear. He said he didn't care if it was black or white, just as long as we all agreed.

When he left, a heated debate began. Veterans like Chuck Howley and Bob Lilly said the white shoes were "sissy" and voted for black. The wild young guys, like running back Mike Montgomery and wide receiver Billy Parks, both traded to us from the Chargers, were adamant about their white shoes. We were deadlocked. Rumor had it that Parks even had white shoes written into his contract! So we voted and decided to let everyone wear whatever he wanted.

Coach Landry came back to the room and we told him our decision. He, as usual, showed no emotion, but we knew that he was disappointed. Over the course of the year, youth prevailed, and we all ultimately changed to white shoes. So much for the good old tough days—times (and shoes) were a-changin'!

CHARLIE'S TALE

The Smoozer

Cornell Green excelled in the NFL for 14 years, making All-Pro at both corner and strong safety. Athletically, he was impressive, but Cornell's most celebrated attributes were his common sense and survival skills.

My first year with the Dallas Cowboys, I was being groomed to replace him at the strong safety position when he retired. Though I desperately wanted to play, there was no competition or animosity between us. We were, and still are, great friends. Cornell was the man. I knew it, respected it, and attempted to learn as much as I possibly could from him. He loved "coaching" me, but more than that, he loved having me take his reps in practice. The hardest part about practice for Cornell was getting dressed, because his stunt man (me) did all of the hard work. I had no problem with that. I was eager and knew that the experience in practice would help me later.

Cornell also helped in the classroom. Coach Landry was a stickler for detail and demanded knowledge of his system. He grilled us with questions about formation tendencies, responsibilities, and keys. It was embarrassing to answer one of his questions wrong in the meeting in front of the entire team. Cornell always seemed to have the right answers and I didn't.

One meeting at training camp, Coach Landry asked me to give him my "keys" for a split formation. Keys, if read properly, tell you who does what at the snap and give you a jump on executing your job. A misread key could result in disaster. Coach Landry left nothing to chance. A split formation had specific keys that telegraphed the play and my

Cornell Green, a Utah basketball player, performed for 14 years and really knew how to work the system.
Photo courtesy of Russ Russell

answer, "The backs," was not one of them. Coach Landry asked Cornell to "straighten this rookie out."

"T…G…O…and Flow, Coach," answered Cornell, with an air of confidence. His answer threw me, because in a game situation it was nearly impossible to look at, and see, the "T" (tackle), "G" (guard), "O" (off guard) and "Flow" (the backs crossing the backfield) at the same time. I was discouraged and thought, "I'll never be able to play this position with all of these keys!"

When the meeting was over, Cornell's tutoring sharpened when he grabbed me and pulled me over to the side and said, "Stunt man, listen to me. T, G, O and Flow is what you answer Coach Landry in the meetings. Memorize what he wants to hear for each formation and answer him."

"But how on earth do you see T, G, O, and Flow all at the snap?" I asked.

"I don't," he answered. "T, G, O, and Flow is Tom's answer, not mine. I just look to see if the quarterback hands the ball off to the back. If he does, then it's a run, and if not, it's a pass. Simple."

CHAPTER 2

Dynamic Duo

CLIFF'S TALE Brain Waves

Teamwork is the most critical component in winning football games, especially in the Landry system. The legendary head coach of the Packers and Landry's mentor, Vince Lombardi, once said, "Teamwork is what the Green Bay Packers were all about. They didn't do it for individual glory. They did it because they loved one another."

Landry's Flex defense had pounded into our heads that there could be no individualism—the "team" won. Each day in our chalk sessions we studied how our individual roles related to the players around us. We saw how we could shut down the strengths of a certain offense, whether it was a potent running attack or a specific speedy receiver, by focusing the Flex on them—and it worked.

Charlie and I had a unique bond. Though we were very competitive with each other, we worked together very well, like no tandem on the Cowboys ever has. I truly felt that Charlie, at times, knew what I was thinking. We had an edge over most people because we were friends and had similar football backgrounds. We had both played quarterback and other positions in the secondary before we reached the pros. We had a thorough understanding of the inner workings of the "system." I had played cornerback throughout high school and college, and even though Charlie hadn't played DB very much in his younger days, he picked it up fast. He was smart and athletic. When I left to go into the army and fulfill my military obligation, Charlie took over my position at free safety and did a good job.

The next season I was back, and Landry moved him out to corner. His best position was not cornerback, and he had a couple of tough years, but his experience and knowledge of the position ultimately helped us relate and coordinate coverages.

Coaches sometimes visualize themselves in certain positions. Coach Landry was a defensive back. I think Landry could see himself in Charlie and wanted him to make it there. Landry was determined to prove that you could play if you could think.

Like Landry, Charlie was a smart and savvy player who relied on the strengths of our structured defensive scheme to back up his shortcomings and enhance his strengths. He relied on me and the other guys in the secondary to be in exactly the positions Landry drew up on the chalkboard. Charlie was a great athlete, but he was not blessed with great speed. He was not designed as a corner, but he did make All-Pro several times at strong safety. Throughout his career, he really used the Flex system to his benefit, particularly at corner.

A great example of our psychic teamwork power was in a game we played in Dallas against the Seattle Seahawks. Jim Zorn was the Seattle quarterback. Charlie and I both knew Jim from the time he spent with the Cowboys a few years before and therefore knew what to expect from him.

In one particular series we had the Seahawks backed up to about their own 20-yard line. Jim dropped back to pass and tried to look me off by looking at the wide receiver on the strong side. It didn't work, because I knew he had his primary receiver running an "in" route from the weak side. I faked as if I were going strong, then immediately switched back to cover the weak side route. I saw the look on Jim's face as he threw the ball. He must have thought, "Oh no! Cliff has got me. I thought I had him going strong." I liked to see that look in a QB.

When he released the ball, I broke and picked it off at about their 30-yard line in the middle of the field and headed full speed toward the sideline and then the end zone. Jim and the rest of the enemy team saw me pick it off and started heading in my direction to stop me. I dodged a few guys, but I saw them closing in on me when I was at about the seven- or eight-yard line. I made a move and cut back into them toward the inside. At the last second, I spun around and flipped the ball into the air. I don't know how I knew, but I felt Charlie there. Instead of leading the blocking for me, he was running behind me. He never said anything to me. I just knew he was there.

As the ball was floating in the air toward Charlie, a surge of Seahawks piled on me, trying to punish me for my interception. It didn't work. Charlie caught my lateral in midair and was

Charlie and Cliff never lost sight of how much fun it was to play in the NFL. ***Photo courtesy of Cowboys Weekly***

sprinting for the end zone. By the time the guys who were trying to hurt me realized what was going on, it was too late. He scored.

Charlie asked me later how I knew he was there. I told him, "Brain waves!"

CHARLIE'S TALE

Necessary Roughness

Joe Theismann is a guy whom I probably would have liked and maybe would've wanted to be my quarterback if he'd played on my team. But he didn't. So I didn't like him. I didn't like his arrogance, his cockiness, or his lack of respect for defensive players. Hating Joe came easy 'cause he played for the Dreaded Evil Empire, the Washington Redskins. Today we are mutually respected friends who shared a colorful, competitive past. I like Joe now, but I think most of Dallas still hates him.

So in 1978 when he took the snap on the last play of the game at RFK Stadium during a *Monday Night Football* broadcast, I was fuming. The Redskins held a comfortable six-point lead, 9-3, and the line of scrimmage for that last play was the Washington 15-yard line—near the end zone where the fans were virtually on top of us. RFK was absolutely the best place to play professional football in the NFL; the fans were rabid and vocal and they hated the Cowboys. It was the opening game of the season, and that night we were sacrificed to the delight of the delirious faithful.

Joe took the snap and retreated backward. He had been instructed to take a safety, giving up the two points by retreating to the end zone. I'm sure he had also been instructed to waste as much time as he could, then step out of the back of the end zone.

He successfully burned out the clock by scooting around in the end zone, but failed to step out of bounds. He pranced around back there, got caught up in the moment and held the ball up in the air—taunting us. That worked the fans into a frenzy.

I was the first Cowboy to get to Theismann. I grabbed him and spun him around, keeping him from going out of the back of the end zone. I also kept him upright. In an attempt to strip

Pesky Joe Theismann, the 'Skins QB Cowboy fans loved to hate. ***Photo courtesy of Cowboys Weekly***

him of the ball, I held on to him with one hand and frantically swiped at the football with the other. Help arrived in the form of Randy White, who exploded into both Theismann and me. He, too, was trying to dislodge the ball. Boy, "The Manster" (half man, half monster) could deliver a blow! Joe miraculously held on to the ball. The referee finally blew the whistle, ending the play and the game. Of course, a fight broke out because Joe's offensive linemen didn't take kindly to Randy and me abusing their leader. It was a short brawl, involving six players from each team. No one got hurt, but the fans smelled blood. I was comforted by the fact that the security guards wouldn't allow them onto the field.

The officials broke up the ruckus. Defeated, we walked to the back of the end zone toward the ramp to our locker room. The noise was deafening.

The tunnel was in a dugout that bordered that end zone. RFK was a classic old baseball stadium that doubled as a football field. The dugout was below field level. The fans spilled over to the top of the dugout. Still in full gear, I focused my attention on carefully negotiating the concrete steps with my steel cleats. That's when the beer bottle exploded on my helmet and beer doused my face and neck, pieces of glass flying everywhere. I looked up and made eye contact with the attacker, still holding the neck of the shattered bottle. He was probably some congressman, venting his alter ego. He taunted, "Yeah, big guy, that was me. You want some of this?" gesturing for me to come up. I think he felt safe in the stands.

I scouted the area for security and noticed that my partner Cliff Harris had witnessed the assault. He had fire in his eyes. He said, "Let's go get him!" And that's just what we did. We climbed up on top of the dugout and launched ourselves right into the midst of the Washington fans, fists flailing. They couldn't retaliate because our armor protected us.

We bloodied as many as we could before two security guards literally dragged us out of the melee by our ankles. Cliff and I exchanged elated high-fives as we scurried up the tunnel to the dressing room.

There were no fines, no lawsuits, no suspensions—no repercussions whatsoever. And thank goodness there were no cameras.

CLIFF'S TALE *Cardiac Cardinals*

People have asked me over the years which of my games were the most exciting or which games I enjoyed the most. The obvious answer is a Super Bowl, because that is the ultimate game—that is what we play for. Though from a pure enjoyment standpoint, that was not always the case. To me, some of the games leading up to the Super Bowl were just as significant and exciting as the big game, but none were ever as overwhelming. Charlie and I both have played in many memorable games. Strangely, I always enjoyed playing on the other guy's turf—away games—and the more tense and hostile the environment, the better. The best was when something was on the line.

Many games in RFK stadium were that way. They were always electrifying because both the Redskins' fans and players hated us so much that we felt like Christians in the Roman Coliseum—we were just waiting for the lions.

How can I compare the Super Bowls to any other games? They, of course, had so much hoopla and worldwide build-up that they were in a class of games all their own. Besides the games at RFK, there is one game that really stands out more than any other. I have heard Charlie mention this same game as his favorite as well. Thanksgiving Day games were also special big games. There was something about playing on Thanksgiving that was unique; maybe it was because it was in the fall and that traditionally means football. The games were always fun and exciting, and you knew, as a player, that all of your NFL contemporaries were at home, relaxing and taking a break from their own wars. They were at their tables eating some turkey and watching

Babyface Jim Hart guided the Cardiac Cardinals.
Photo courtesy of Cowboys Weekly

you perform on TV. That was added pressure, so we had to perform well.

We played in several of those Turkey Day games, but my favorite is a game played in Texas Stadium against the St. Louis Cardinals in the middle of Charlie's and my careers. That year, both teams were in the running for the division championship, fighting our way to the Super Bowl. Babyface (as he was referred to by the press) Jim Hart, the great veteran quarterback for the Cardinals, had brought his team back from behind in the fourth quarter to win in each of their last six games. The press had anointed them the "Cardiac Cards." They were definitely on a hot streak.

That Thanksgiving Day was unseasonably warm, as I remember. The afternoon sun was shining through the hole in the roof of Texas Stadium, which made seeing the ball sometimes difficult. With the early afternoon game, people at home were probably finishing their pumpkin pie and settling on their couches for some football. Texas Stadium was filled to the brim and buzzing with electricity from all the folks who had missed out on turkey to watch "The Boys" play. During the national anthem, both teams were lined up, facing each other, on the sidelines, anxious, tuned and ready to go. When the ref blew his whistle and pulled his arm down to signal "Let's roll," my stomach flopped. I knew that day was going to be a real test.

We had the ball first, and I had enormous confidence in Roger Staubach. No one in football could win like Rog, but somehow today I knew it was going to be up to the defense to capture the victory. The Cards were having a very good year and were playing us extremely tough. They had never been to a Super Bowl and were hungry. We always seemed to be the dead end to their postseason road. By the fourth quarter we had not put them completely away. The fans were anxious; you could feel the nervous tension in the stadium.

Like their previous games, it was the fourth quarter with two minutes left and the Cards still had a shot. They were only four points behind. We had the ball and just needed to hold onto it for two short minutes. We were around our own 30-yard line, and it looked as if we had the game in the bag. On second down we ran a sweep play. Unbelievably, the ball popped out of our running back's hands, right to one of the Cardinal defenders. The defensive guys resting on the bench, thinking we had the victory in our hands, grabbed our helmets, jumped up and ran onto the field. We all knew we had to really step up our intensity.

As both teams were huddling, Jimmy Hart looked up and we exchanged glances. Our eyes met and he smiled slyly. He was sending me a signal that said, "Now we've got you!" On the first play, Jim handed the ball off to their tough fullback, Jim Otis, and he made a few yards. Now the Cards were on our 33-yard line—third and four. This was a gray area for a defensive coordinator calling our next defense. Percentage-wise, the Cards were 50/50 running or passing in that situation. Ernie Stautner usually leaned towards stopping the run, which meant we would not have a very good pass rush.

Sure enough, he signaled in a run defense. We lined up, the ball was snapped, and naturally…it was a pass.

Jim Hart was not only a smart QB, but also a very accurate and poised passer. His favorite target was Mel Gray, one of the fastest men in pro football. Jim's favorite route was the up-route right along the sideline to Gray about 20 yards downfield. It was a very difficult route for the cornerback to cover and even harder for me to help from my position in the middle of the field.

I anticipated that route and took off for the sideline. Gray was flying, and I was closing in on him. Our cornerback, Benny Barnes, was a step behind, chasing him. Jim lobbed a perfect pass and it was falling right into Gray's hands. I hit him with all that I had at the instant he touched the ball. He flew backwards out of bounds and landed on his back. I was on top of him, face to face. The look on Mel Gray's face when he sat up, looked right into my eyes, held the ball up and smiled, said, "I caught it. We've really got you now!"

The catch put the Cards on our 12-yard line with less than two minutes to go. They had four shots at the end zone. I couldn't have asked for more pressure than that!

Jim Hart had his team right where he wanted them—a very potent offense with three great receivers and an incredible running back in Terry Metcalf.

The next series of plays will always be etched in my mind. On the first three downs, Jim Hart threw passes into the end zone, and either Charlie or I knocked them down and incomplete. Then came the deciding moment. On fourth down, Jim and the Cards felt the weight of all those years of coming in second to the Cowboys and never making it to the Super Bowl. Now was their chance! There were only 18 seconds left on the clock.

The ball was snapped to Jim and he dropped back. His outside receivers took off on crossing routes from one side of the field to the other. It was Hart's last chance. He fired a spiral toward the middle of the field. I saw the ball coming as if in slow motion. In the split second before it reached the hands of the receiver, I leaped and slapped the ball away. At the same instant, Charlie, coming from the other side, blasted receiver J.V. Cain, who was frozen at

Cliff and Charlie on the last-second double-team.
Photo courtesy of Dick Wittingham

the goal line waiting for the Hart TD pass. As the ball fell incomplete, their comeback streak screeched to a halt. We were on our way to the Super Bowl, and the Cards were headed home—again.

CLIFF'S TALE *Double Vision*

Charlie and I used to wonder what the TV or radio commentators might be saying at certain times during our games. There were times when one of our cornerbacks was beaten deep on a touchdown pass, and even though our responsibility was short coverage, we sometimes saw the play coming and took off deep in an attempt to break it up. It may have been a great play to just get close enough to help out, but to the camera, it looked like we missed. And probably, we were the ones who received the blame for allowing the TD. The CB may have been beaten so badly that he was not even in the TV screen at all. We wondered if the all-knowing announcers said, "Cliff Harris (or Charlie Waters) was just beaten deep on a great route by the receiver," when they really did not know who was responsible for what. Sometimes things were not as they seemed.

Charlie did not have good vision until after his recent laser surgery. During his playing days he had an astigmatism and could not see at a distance without his contacts. His contacts were new-age technology at the time and were specially designed for his unique vision impairment. The lenses of his contacts were not the normal circular disks, but were actually oval shaped and weighted at one end to achieve proper lens alignment. It was a good product for a normal person, but not necessarily for a pro football player who often got hit in the head so hard that it rattled his eyes. They were not designed to take a jolt, and sometimes his lenses were knocked off center. When that happened, Charlie could not see anything. It was like he was looking through the end of a Coke bottle.

One fall afternoon in the new Meadowlands Stadium in New Jersey, we were playing the New York Giants. It was a beautiful day for a game—clear, cool and sunny, about 50 degrees. In the first series, Charlie went up and made a great tackle at the line of scrimmage. When he hit the running back, it spun the contacts in his eyes out of alignment. Everything was blurry and he couldn't see anything.

We had a contingency plan ready, though. When Charlie got up from the tackle he yelled for me to come over and help him. I ran over and got right in his face and looked at his contacts. As the offense and defense were huddling up and calling the next play, Charlie and I were huddled trying to bring his vision back. Instead of the weighted ends being at the bottom of his irises at a six o'clock position, one was turned about 45 degrees and the other was about 60 degrees off center.

The Meadowlands is a very noisy stadium. The crowd was going crazy and it was extremely loud on the field. Charlie couldn't hear me at all. I screamed for him to turn his right contact 45 degrees in a counterclockwise direction. He did not know if I meant his right or my right. It was a fiasco. The clock was ticking. The Giants were about to break the huddle any second. It would not work to have a blind DB running around. Finally, I pointed to one of his eyes, then pointed which direction the contact should be turned. He understood and, with his finger, turned the contact in one eye correctly. He could see, thanks to good communication! We did the same for the other eye, and he was back in business. The offense broke the huddle and we lined up in our positions. We didn't miss a beat!

We had to do that several times during games, and we became very proficient. Another little complication came when Charlie had "stickum" on his fingers to help him catch passes and he had to touch his fragile contacts. In pro football you learn how to respond to all kinds of challenges!

We laughed later and wondered what the announcers might have said about our antics—me standing in Charlie's face pointing my fingers in different directions. I am sure that whatever they said, they did not get it right!

CHARLIE'S TALE

Butterflies

I believe that the very best moment in sports is the pregame warmup. It represents the final preparation and the game is imminent—no more waiting. The time to fight is near.

When I was in the NFL, it took two days to recover after the last game, and on Wednesday we started a steady ascent to reach a crescendo on Sunday. I loved the inevitability of a game. There are few circumstances that will cancel or postpone a football game, unlike baseball. That's why the pregame warmup, one hour before the game, was so dear to my heart.

Anticipation can be misconstrued as nervousness. Butterflies in your stomach are what all athletes feel before they compete. Of course the Super Bowl produces the ultimate butterflies. Two weeks of pregame analysis brings both teams to a fevered pitch. But the same butterflies that invade the guts of an eight-year-old before his first at-bat in baseball are the exact same butterflies that migrate to the Super Bowl. All athletes get them. It's the one thing we all share, no matter what level we are competing at.

In 1975, our third Super Bowl in six years, I was ready to play again the first day after the NFC championship game, so by game day the magical pregame warmup was a relief and a

Franco Harris's mammoth size belied his weaving running style. ***Photo courtesy of Cowboys Weekly***

welcome remedy for a bad case of butterflies. On the first series against Pittsburgh in Miami, Super Bowl X, the butterflies were still lingering. A sure-fire way to run them off is to have a serious collision. The force of the contact literally knocks them out, and the Super Bowl becomes just another game.

Six plays into the first drive, I had not been at the point of contact. On the seventh play, Pittsburgh set the backs in a split formation. I aligned myself on the tight end and timed my attack to the cadence of Terry Bradshaw. The defense was called "Flex Weak Storm," translated to mean: weak side alignment for the defensive strength and all linebackers and the strong safety were blitzing or attacking the line of scrimmage in the gaps between the line. There would be no hole to run.

It was an excellent run-situation blitz, best versus first-down situations because the Steelers had a 70:30 run-to-pass ratio. My pass responsibility was the fullback on my side if he elected to release on a route rather than block. I should have known that the back lined up on my side was not there to be a lead blocker. It was Franco Harris. He was big enough to be a lead blocker, but he was never used in that capacity. I knew that, but the butterflies blocked my logic and vision.

I timed my surge perfectly as Terry barked the signals and center Mike Webster snapped the ball. Looking to collide with someone to get rid of those butterflies, I charged at Franco's outside shoulder. I was also hoping to turn the running play back into one of the linebackers.

The problem was that it was not a running play. Franco deftly avoided my bull-like charge that would rival the best matadors in Spain. He slipped me and headed to the flat, but then rounded into a swing route, about seven yards past the line of scrimmage and clinging to the sideline.

I was frozen in no man's land. When I realized it was a pass, I was too late to catch Franco. But rather than rush Bradshaw, I turned and watched as Terry's ball sailed over my head and dropped perfectly into Franco's stomach. He looked the ball in, just as he was taught, so he didn't see the blur coming from the middle of the field.

Simultaneously, the cavalry (Cliff) arrived at the same time the ball did to save the fort (my butt) just in the nick of time. With perfect timing, my buddy Cliff Harris had saved me. Captain Crash smashed into Franco about chest high with the velocity of a freight train, not only knocking the ball loose from Franco's grasp, but jarring his helmet sideways on his head as he slid into the mass of cameramen lining the sidelines.

The butterflies in my stomach were gone. The fear over that misread had driven them away.

In the postgame summary, that heart-stopping play was described simply as an incomplete pass thanks to Cliff. That's what friends are for.

CLIFF'S TALE

Seeing Stars

Charlie Waters and I made a good combination. We each knew where the other was at all times on the field and relied on each other's strengths to make big plays and help win games. We were there when we needed each other. This was particularly true one day in Texas Stadium when we played the Cincinnati Bengals. It was toward the end of the season and we were working our way into the playoffs and hopefully the Super Bowl. The Bengals had a good team that year, and at halfback they had a really tough guy named Boobie Clark who weighed about 240 pounds.

We were ahead in the third quarter and it was a close game. To put a halt to any Cincinnati momentum, we

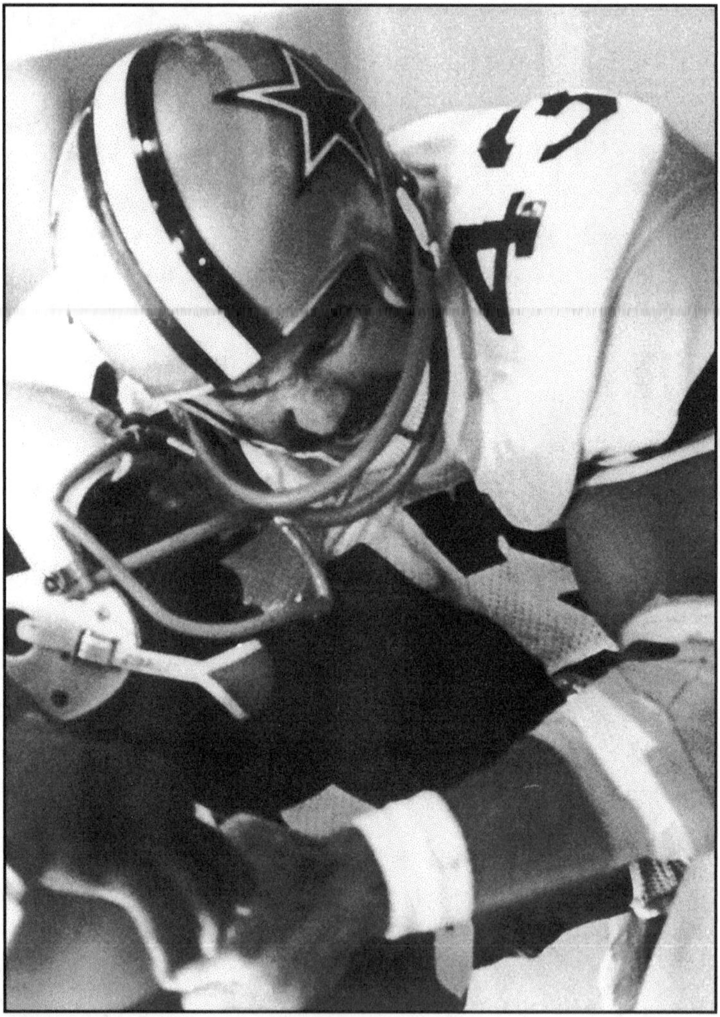

Sparks fly—collisions were Cliff's game.
Photo courtesy of Cowboys Weekly

needed to stop the savvy Bengals QB Ken Anderson and his offense on third and one. The Dallas crowd in Texas Stadium was going berserk. A blitz was signaled in from the sidelines from our defensive coordinator, Ernie Stautner, and Lee Roy Jordan relayed the call into the huddle—4-3 Storm blitz. That meant that Lee Roy and D.D. Lewis, our weak-side linebacker, were blitzing, and my job was to cover the fullback. I had Boobie wherever he went; pass or run, he was my responsibility.

The Bengals came out in a spread formation instead of a normal third-and-short double-tight end formation. The spread allowed the Bengals the flexibility to pass or run. I tried my best not to give the blitz away by not lining up too close to the line of scrimmage, but I also wanted to be close enough to make sure Anderson didn't hit Boobie on a quick short pass. They snapped the ball, and I read the play quickly. It was a running play, right up the gut to Boobie. There was a wide hole, and I met Boobie head on at the line of scrimmage. The lights went out and bells rang; that was the last thing I remember. The next thing I remember, I was looking around at unfamiliar surroundings. It was as if I were in a dream. I felt detached from reality. I recognized that I was playing football, but I wasn't exactly sure about the other details. I finally wandered over to our huddle and found Charlie. I told him I didn't know where I was or whom we were playing. He pointed to the ground and said, "Cliff, see that line?"

"Yeah."

"Follow it." The line led to our sidelines and safety. Thanks, Charlie. I hope I can return the favor some day.

CHARLIE'S TALE *TKOed*

Cliff Harris was a hit man—a kamikaze pilot who usually sank his target upon collision. Difference was, he lived to do it again and again. The NFL record for most opponents KOed in a row is proudly held by Cliff. Jack Tatum of the Raiders and Ronnie Lott of the 49ers are distant seconds.

Every game, Tom Landry and his braintrust would set a game plan. Along with a tactical plan, the coach would also name three priorities for the defense to concentrate on. The defense had to take care of those three concerns in order to win. Two of the three goals were usually strategy-related, and the third was usually an individual target—a star wide receiver, a magical quarterback, or a speedy running back.

All professional players have a special way to prepare themselves for game day. Cliff's game preparation, along with intensely studying the opposition, was fueled by passion. It was important for Cliff to dislike the opponent, even if he knew him. Actually, "dislike" is too kind. Cliff worked up a hatred that peaked on game day, and he usually targeted one player.

On January 1, 1978, Dallas Cowboys versus Minnesota Vikings in the national conference divisional playoff game at Texas Stadium, Tom Landry announced that the second defensive goal was to stop wide receiver Ahmad Rashad.

That was all Cliff needed: a target. During the week he worked hard to build a sincere hatred for Rashad. Cliff had a problem though; he couldn't get past a friendship he had formed with Ahmad at the Pro Bowl the previous year.

Cliff values his friends, and Rashad was a friend. But Cliff met him before he had embraced Islam and changed his name from Bobby Moore to Ahmad Rashad. Cliff reconciled his dilemma with this rationale: his friend is Bobby Moore, not Ahmad Rashad.

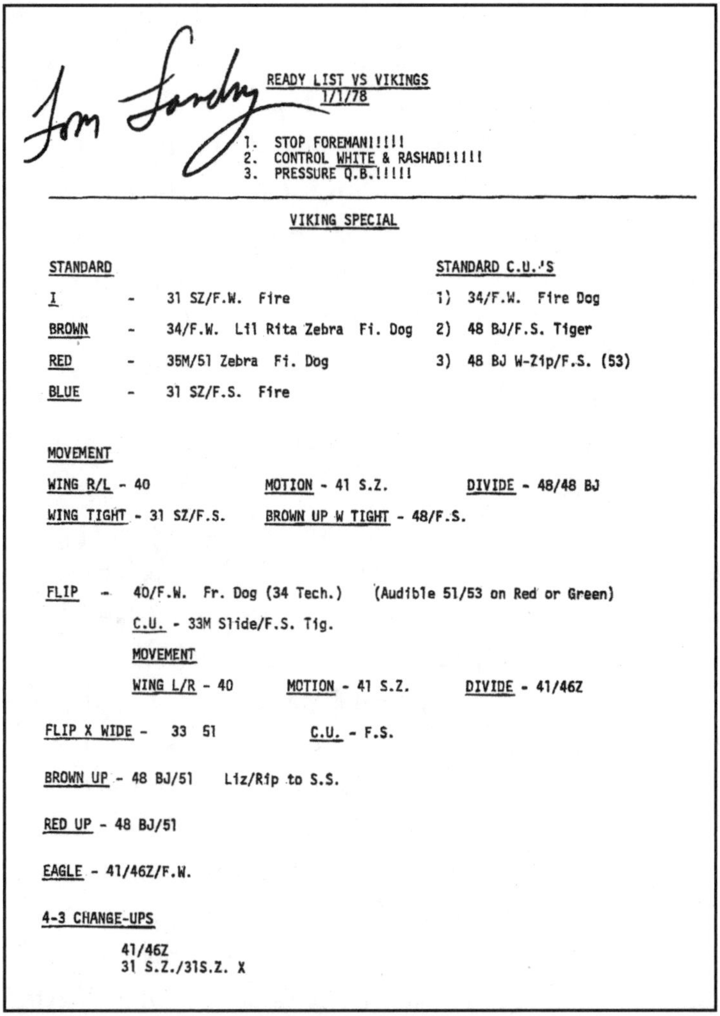

Tom Landry

READY LIST VS VIKINGS
1/1/78

1. STOP FOREMAN!!!!!
2. CONTROL WHITE & RASHAD!!!!!
3. PRESSURE Q.B.!!!!!

VIKING SPECIAL

STANDARD

I - 31 SZ/F.W. Fire
BROWN - 34/F.W. Lil Rita Zebra Fi. Dog
RED - 35M/51 Zebra Fi. Dog
BLUE - 31 SZ/F.S. Fire

STANDARD C.U.'S

1) 34/F.W. Fire Dog
2) 48 BJ/F.S. Tiger
3) 48 BJ W-Zip/F.S. (53)

MOVEMENT

WING R/L - 40 MOTION - 41 S.Z. DIVIDE - 48/48 BJ
WING TIGHT - 31 SZ/F.S. BROWN UP W TIGHT - 48/F.S.

FLIP - 40/F.W. Fr. Dog (34 Tech.) (Audible 51/53 on Red or Green)
C.U. - 33M Slide/F.S. Tig.
MOVEMENT
WING L/R - 40 MOTION - 41 S.Z. DIVIDE - 41/46Z

FLIP X WIDE - 33 51 C.U. - F.S.

BROWN UP - 48 BJ/51 Liz/Rip to S.S.

RED UP - 48 BJ/51

EAGLE - 41/46Z/F.W.

4-3 CHANGE-UPS

41/46Z
31 S.Z./31S.Z. X

Page one of three of a Doomsday game plan—signed by the creator. ***Courtesy of Cliff Harris***

"I got it!" he announced to me. "I hate Ahmad Rashad. That's different than hating Bobby Moore. New name, new person…no friendship! I hate Ahmad Rashad!" He was ready.

The first play from scrimmage in that playoff game with Minnesota featured a slot formation—two wide receivers on the same side, with Rashad at the inside position. The route was a deceptive, high-risk play designed to burn our defense early. A three-step drop by the quarterback alerted the whole defense that the route would be short, but that was, in fact, a misread. Both receivers ran a short crossing route, with Rashad slanting to the outside. Our corner, Aaron Kyle was covering Rashad. He read the three-step set and jumped on the short out-route.

Quarterback Bob Lee pumped and Kyle bit. Rashad turned up the field and also turned on the jets. It was a trick—a counter route—commonly known as a pump-and-go. Fooled, Kyle was way out of the picture, but he was struggling to recover. To Lee, it appeared that Rashad was loose, flying down the sideline.

How sick would we be if Doomsday gave up a huge, big-time play right out of the chute? Lee reset his feet, cocked his arm, and floated a 30-yard pass downfield toward Rashad, who was hugging the sideline. Cliff had played in the league for many years, and his experience served him well. When he saw Bob Lee set, he instinctively knew that he had no intention of throwing that short route. So Cliff, rather than taking the bait on the three-step fake, directed his energies toward the area where the ball would end up. Like a heat-seeking missile, Cliff dialed in the coordinates for the point of contact. He took the absolute perfect angle to reach his explosion point at exactly the instant the ball would drop into Rashad's hands.

He never considered going for an interception. He was focused on goal number two in the game plan: Control White and Rashad. I had a mental picture of a goggled Cliff in the cockpit, leather helmet, earflaps flopping in the wind, throwing down a shot of sake, sacrificing for his team—pure kamikaze.

The collision was vintage Cliff "Captain Crash" Harris. He left his feet about four yards before contact and exploded with everything he had into and through Rashad's chest, shoulders, chin and face.

The force of the impact ricocheted through Rashad and also claimed Kyle, the corner, who had recovered from the fake and was now near the area of impact. Too bad for Aaron; he was in Cliff's crosshairs and was a victim of collateral damage.

Helmets, wrist bands, shoes, elbow pads, chin straps, mouthpieces and blood flew everywhere. When the dust settled, Cliff stood up and assessed the bomb site for survivors. Both Viking Rashad and Cowboy Kyle were out cold. Their limp bodies lay three yards apart, out of bounds. Kyle was face down and Rashad on his back, helmet partially dislodged from his head.

Cliff walked closer and gestured for me to come over and share the moment. When I arrived, both teams already had their training crews at work trying to revive the still bodies.

Ahmad's face was calm. He had a gash on his chin, but his nose was still in place. There was, though, a massive wad of snot, dirt and spit that covered his face and drooled over his cheeks. I knew Ahmad was still with us, because when he breathed through his nose a small bubble formed and settled on his upper lip. The classic snot bubble—a rare sight in pro sports.

Cliff asked me rather innocently, "Hey, Charlie, is this Ahmad Rashad or Bobby Moore?"

Check. One of our three defensive goals was accomplished, because whatever name he was going by, he was out for the rest of the game.

CLIFF'S TALE

"Let's Go With It!"

As I have mentioned, injuries were a part of the game, and as players we learned to live with them. Charlie Waters had more than his fair share. During my football career I was very fortunate and had only one operation—on my knee. My freshman year in college, my own teammate hit me and tore my cartilage—the medial meniscus. A knee operation then was a four-inch zipper, not today's pinpoint arthroscopic surgery. My operation took place over Easter, and I recovered enough to run track later that year.

Charlie was not so lucky. He has had six or seven operations on his knees, not to mention other various operations on his ankles and shoulders. Today he has five vertebrae in his back fused, with a metal rod holding his spine in place. He is a bit hobbled and just had his knee joint replaced with a titanium ball and socket. Football is a rough sport!

One nearly career-ending injury happened to Charlie on the AstroTurf of the Seattle Seahawks' Kingdome in the preseason of our 10th year. As you would expect, most injuries occur during the collision of bodies during tremendous hits, tackles, or blocks. Charlie's injury, though, took place when no one was around him. We had called a coverage, 33 Wing, that isolated him on the tight end, man to man. When the ball was snapped, Charlie was backpedaling, covering the receiver as he took off downfield on his route. The big tight end then made his quick cut from the post to the corner route. Charlie recognized and reacted to the route and turned to break with him, but his cleats stayed locked into the turf and the twist on his knee tore his ACL. He says he stepped on a landmine.

He collapsed on the field into a pile and immediately grabbed his knee. When I saw him, I had a sick feeling. If it was what I thought, he could be out for a long time, and maybe for his career. With my partner Charlie gone, football was not as much fun for me. That, combined with a neck injury of my own, gave me reason to retire at the end of that season. I thought Charlie was through, too. He busted his tail in rehab, though, and made a miraculous comeback the next year. I had already retired, but Charlie was a tough-minded, comeback kind of guy.

His real comeback had already happened years before. Early in our careers, we returned punts together. He and I were twin return men, both back deep on punts—one catching and the other blocking. Whoever the ball came closest to was the one who caught it and ran it back while the other blocked for him. When the ball was between us, I made the call on who would take it.

We were playing the Skins in RFK. It was early December, and the NFC championship game, with a Super Bowl berth, was at stake. A win would mean that in our first three years in the NFL, Charlie and I would have played in three Super Bowls. Nobody had ever done that. It was a late afternoon game that went into the evening. You could not describe a better football environment for a championship game. RFK was exploding, with the 55,000 fans going crazy as usual. It was an old, dark, brick stadium, but it was full of rowdy and intense fans. It was a typical cold fall afternoon in the northeast. The field was real grass, but most of the turf had been worn off, leaving mainly dirt, which was spray-painted green for the TV audience. That night was destined to be one of those memorable games.

The Redskins had one of the best specialty teams in the league—definitely the toughest.

It was the end of the fourth quarter and the score was 21-17. Charlie and I were lined up and ready back at our own 40-yard line. Roger and the offense had not done much all day. We needed a touchdown. There were only a few minutes left, so right before the punt, I told Charlie that we needed a spark to get us going. I said, "We aren't going to fair-catch the ball and we have to make something happen, so let's go with it—no matter what!" He nodded and I thought, "Here we go."

The ball was punted and it drifted toward Charlie. It was not a very long or high punt, which meant, like a pack of hungry wolves, the wild specialty team guys were sprinting downfield as Charlie was watching the ball into his hands. There were about four or five guys closing in on him. I did my best to block as many as I could. He really had no chance, and in any other situation he should have fair-caught it.

He was hit by one of the guys I couldn't block, and then another. He shifted to his left and was hit by another. He spun and put his left hand to the ground to regain his balance. With all of Charlie's weight on his extended left arm, a would-be tackler put his shoulder right into Charlie's elbow. I heard a rifle-shot sound, then heard Charlie scream. I looked over at the pile of bodies and saw Charlie writhing on the ground. The bone was sticking out of the upper part of his arm. I thought, "Oh, man! He is done." It was a compound fracture of his humerus, the second largest bone in the body. I am still amazed that he managed to hold onto the football.

Our medical staff was on the field immediately to attend to Charlie. I knelt next to him until Dr. Marvin Knight and company took over. Old-school Dr. Knight addressed Charlie's injured left arm by grabbing his hand. Then with his left hand, Dr. Knight reached up and stabilized Charlie's left shoulder. I thought he was just analyzing the extent of the break when I heard this blood-curdling scream. I almost passed out as I witnessed Dr. Knight set Charlie's arm at the 35-yard line at RFK Stadium, in the dirt, with nothing for the pain.

Trainers Don Cochran and Larry Gardner, after stabilizing the arm in a pressurized air cast, helped Charlie off the field.

We lost the game, and it was a long flight home, especially for Charlie.

I went in to see him in the hospital. He looked bad, and after a couple of weeks he had lost a lot of weight and muscle tone. I thought his career was over, but he surprised

Trainer Larry Gardner assisted as tough-ass team doctor Marvin Knight set Charlie's arm at the 35-yard line.
Photo courtesy of Cowboys Weekly

everyone and worked hard in the off-season. He came back the next year. Landry moved him from corner to safety, and after all that, he made All-Pro a few years later. I would not have bet that he would be back, but Charlie proved everyone wrong—more than once.

CHARLIE'S TALE

Nightmare

I was amazed that Dr. Knight set my broken bone on the field at RFK. His Korean War experience not only toughened him, it taught him plenty, also.

Of course, I spent the night with my arm in traction in a Dallas hospital under the assumption that an operation was imminent the next day. Dr. Knight, with his familiar cowboy hat on, arrived in my room the next day with my X-rays. Doctors love to show you X-rays, but I could never tell what I was looking at. He pointed out how close the two halves of the humerus were aligned. Setting the bones so soon after the break—though not aligned perfectly—had remarkably initiated healing already. I got the speech about how the bone would ultimately be stronger than its original state, because of the calcium buildup. He volunteered that there were a lot of these "field" settings in Korea.

The recommendation was for me to remain in traction at Baylor Hospital for five more days for safety precautions, but not to do surgery. Before being released from the hospital, they secured my arm in a cast. I was to report for a check-up in four weeks.

Once things began to normalize, a depression came over me, and the reality of the season set in. The only thing that wasn't on a healing path was my psyche. I felt we had lost that championship game because I gave up a touchdown pass to Charley Taylor. Taylor, ultimately a Hall of Famer, was my nightmare. His persona as an intimidating wide receiver worked against the rules of the game. Wide receivers don't intimidate; defensive backs do. As we lay on the end zone

Converted from running back, tough wide receiver Charley Taylor was dangerous both before and after catches.
Photo courtesy of the Washington Redskins

turf, Charley confidently proclaimed, "You'll *never* be able to cover me." The pain of losing was worse than the physical pain. I had to beat my injury; I wanted another shot at Taylor. I had to get well.

Two weeks passed without incident. Then one night I took a rare shower. Showering was difficult. The sling holding the cast in the proper position had to be untied, then my cast had to be wrapped in towels and plastic bags to keep out the moisture. The sling was then re-tied over the cover-up. Showers were normally enjoyable. This one wasn't, though. I was relaxed and loving the hot shower when my newly tied sling loosened itself and my whole left arm—heavy in its cast—snapped down in a freefall. The pain was excruciating. I immediately called the doctor. He said, "Aw, you can't hurt it in that cast. Come see me in two weeks at your scheduled appointment."

The two weeks dragged by and I returned for my check-up. The ashen hue of the doctor's face gave him away immediately, but the first set of X-rays that I could actually read confirmed it. Inside my cast, the two pieces of my humerus were lying next to each other and had started healing sideways.

The jolt in the shower had broken the rough set Dr. Knight performed on game day, and the bones had shifted. The following day I had surgery. They re-broke my arm and set it again. In addition, a 14-inch steel rod was inserted through the bone marrow to keep it in line. The rod had a hook on one end that protruded from my shoulder. It was supposed to make it easier to extract once the break healed. The hooked rod was scheduled to remain for three weeks for alignment reasons until the healing process took over.

After three weeks, I reported back to the doctor—no noticeable healing. The "non-fusion" was a result of the arm being traumatized three times in one month. It was rejecting any and all of nature's healing ways. I couldn't work out—not even running—for fear of jolting my arm. I went from 185 pounds to 165 pounds over the summer. I am sure that worrying about my arm, being haunted by Charley Taylor and dying a thousand deaths over the Washington loss contributed.

The entire off-season went by and my arm wouldn't heal. Three weeks before we were scheduled to report to training camp, I met with Dr. Knight. That day he doubled as an orthopedic specialist and a shrink. I absolutely had to play to redeem myself for the loss at the end of last year. Crusty old Dr. Knight was sympathetic.

Together we determined that I was left with three options:

1. Do nothing and eventually nature would do the healing—probably missing the season.

2. Perform a bone graft by taking bone from my hip and grafting it to my arm. This option would ensure healing, but it would be extremely painful and would take a long time to heal—thus missing most of the season.

3. Or, we could drive the steel rod further into the bone and close the wound and I could possibly play.

Option three was my only option. Dr. Knight secured a couple of nurses, shot some Novocain around the shoulder, and literally hammered the rod down into my arm. He sewed the open wound, closing the skin over the hook.

I played the entire season at left corner, every play, with my left arm broken. It doesn't speak much for my intelligence, but it does say a little more about those of us from that era. We were paid to play, and play we did, if there was any way possible.

I never got hit directly on the left arm the entire year. Playing corner helped as I was removed from collisions most of the time. I could pick my battles. Amazingly I was semi-efficient at tackling, once I got over the fear. There was no pain, except for when the Novocain wore off the night after every game.

As for my retribution, I don't think I ever did cover Charley Taylor (he was right), but we did start dominating Washington again. I ultimately got redemption after a span of several years, when Coach Landry moved me into the strong safety position.

Near the end of our game in Dallas the next year, I intercepted a Redskins pass and taunted their team with the

Escorted by 14-year vet Dave Edwards, Charlie scored the take-control TD against the 'Skins.
Photo courtesy of Cowboys Weekly

ball raised over my head as I scored the take-control-of-the-game touchdown. We held a serious dominance over the evil empire for three straight years following that game.

How sweet it was.

CHAPTER 3

Coach Tom Landry

Little Rules

Discipline won close games; both Cliff and I were convinced. Tom Landry believed in discipline. He was disciplined, and all those who worked for him were disciplined—or they were gone. We players not only held him in awe, we also feared him in a strange way. Why? It was the aura of order and perfection that he projected. His expectations of us planted a fear of unimaginable consequences if we failed, though it wasn't fear of his retribution, it was the fear of disappointing him. We didn't want to let him down, especially with mental mistakes.

His leadership was supported by his self-confidence and self-discipline. He expected a lot from himself, and naturally, he also expected a lot from us. We all immediately respected him, but it took a while for us to earn his respect. Because of that respect, we all "snapped to" when he entered the room. The decibel level always dropped drastically when he visited the training room, which was normally a refuge for us, enlivened by loud exchanges and laughter.

The assistant coaches under Tom Landry were just that, "under" him. He ruled them and they also feared him (except, of course, for Mike Ditka). Coach Landry could and would humiliate them just as badly as he could humiliate us.

Every man on our team was subject to certain rules. It mattered not who you were, you played by the rules—even the little ones. Cliff and I were on board with Coach Landry when it came to discipline. As a matter of fact, we represented a segment of the team that enforced the rules internally. If someone loafed at practice, Cliff or I would catch him off guard with a forearm to the side of his helmet. After a while, those who were not in line eventually got the message. All of Coach Landry's rules were understood and made clear. Broken rules resulted in, first, "calling out" the culprit, which was a lot worse than the dreaded extra running after practice. Often, broken rules resulted in a fine that really hit home. Our small salaries could not support many fines.

Some rules seemed silly or of little importance, but I think he used those to create good habits in us when it came to discipline. Playing by the little rules made it easier to play by the big ones. The big rules could change the outcome of a game.

"No sitting at practice" was one of the many little rules. The rule was broad in nature—no sitting on the bench, no sitting on tackling dummies, no sitting between plays and no sitting allowed by those observing practice. That's right, even the media had to stand for the duration. Now that I think about it, Coach Landry didn't like leaning much, either.

Kneeling on one knee was allowed. But kneeling and propping ourselves up with our helmet was taboo, because another little rule was that our helmet was never to touch the ground, except of course when it was driven there.

Working under the premise that "Perfect Practice Makes Perfect," you would think that on game day, Coach would be the same stickler about the little rules as he was in practice, but for some reason, game days were different. Only the big rules mattered on game day.

I really think Coach Landry wanted us all to be a little less intimidated on game day. He let us play, especially if we followed the rules in practice and paid our dues. He called it "reacting as a football player," which really meant that within the Landry football system, you could take liberties...as long as they worked. Game days were free...well, more free.

So, in a blatant display of insubordination, Cliff and I not only sat down on the sidelines during most games, but we invited double trouble by using our helmets as seats. We were certain TL saw us because we positioned ourselves as close to the first-down marker as we could get so we could still feel the flow of the game while resting. With us plopped down on our helmets, TL veered around us several times to avoid tripping. The Man never said a word to us about it. He just ignored us.

Of course, our defiant expression was made only after we had both made All-Pro and had a combined 18 years of NFL experience. By then he didn't scare us—on game days anyway.

CLIFF'S TALE

Flip Flops

Training camp practices were tough in Thousand Oaks. There were two practices a day. One at 9 a.m., then another at 3 p.m. Our time was tightly controlled. You could not miss or be late to anything. Eating was not mandatory, but we had to check in to the meal on time. Breakfast was from 7 to 8 a.m., lunch was from 12 to 1 p.m., and dinner was from 6 to 7 p.m., followed by a meeting from 7:30 until 9 or 10 p.m. Our days were very regimented. If we were late to anything, we were fined. We had Wednesday and Saturday nights off, with curfews at 11 p.m. and 12 a.m. respectively. Coming in after curfew, which happened to some, often called for fines and extra work.

The practices were a real test. They demanded focus and excellent conditioning. We were measured on just about everything. We were expected to understand football fundamentals, so those were not worked on very much. Most of the work concentrated on honing our skills and perfecting our knowledge and execution of the Landry system. Coach Landry was always looking for an edge over the opponents, whether it was mental, physical, emotional, or psychological. Conditioning was one thing he knew he could control.

We were an extremely well-conditioned team. Conditioning started with a very demanding off-season program, then we worked in the weight program and ran during the season.

There was a saying on the wall in our locker room that read, "Fatigue makes a coward of us all." I think it was one

Armed with his trusty bullhorn, Coach Landry monitors the Thousand Oaks training camp from the tower.
Photo courtesy of Cowboys Weekly

of several Lombardi quotes that we had around the facility. TL wanted to make sure we were in shape. He believed in conditioning and did all he could to get us there. He hired top-notch trainers to design our extensive conditioning programs.

At the end of every practice we ran sprints up and down the field for what seemed like forever. On some days, Tom would instruct us, at the end of our sprints, to do "belly flops"—an exercise invented by the devil himself. A belly flop is just what it sounds like. We would run in place and then, when TL would blow a whistle and say "front," we were expected to extend our arms and lay out, landing only on our bellies, then hop up fast and resume running in place. If he said "back," we were to land on our backs instead. If Tom thought we were catching ourselves with our hands or not running in place full speed, he would penalize us with a timed 440-yard run around the track after flops ended.

I ran the 440 in track at Ouachita, but not in full pads and not after a complete football practice. It was a killer run and I knew it, so I really tried hard to execute my flops perfectly for TL.

One day after practice in our flop session, Tom called me out as a guy who was catching myself before my belly hit the ground. Knowing what happened if you did not go full speed on flops, I could not believe he said that I wasn't. I didn't know why he singled me out. I knew what lay in store for me—a bust-ass quarter. Backs were expected to run the quarter in less than 80 seconds. I was mad, so I sucked it up and got ready to go hard at the penalty run. I'll show him, I thought. It was probably just what he wanted!

After flops, everyone who TL called out lined up on the track that ran around the practice field. I was psyched up and when he said go and clicked his stopwatch, I took off. I really busted it and left everyone else behind. I ran the quarter like I did in the track meets of my past and really kicked hard at the finish. I crossed the finish line where Coach stood, and he could not believe my time. He exclaimed with as much enthusiasm as he could muster, "Cliff, you ran a 52-second quarter." And that was with full pads and after two full practices, plus flops! I was still mad, so I did not stop running. I ran right past him and down the path to the field house and the showers. I don't know what came over me, but he never made me run again. Did he win or did I?

Flower Child

Steve Kiner was a product of the '60s. In stature, the big-play, agile linebacker out of Tennessee was from the mold of the great Lee Roy Jordan. His body type, 6'2", 217 pounds, is where the similarities ended. Lee Roy was a strict, disciplined, no-nonsense follower of Bear Bryant. Steve was a free spirit flower child not far removed from the Hare Krishna. For example, in contrast to the Mercedes Benz and sport utility vehicles most players drove, Steve sported around Dallas in an old, beat-up Volkswagen van adorned with psychedelic scenes of flowers and mushrooms.

Respect for authority was not a major issue on Steve's agenda. All of Coach Landry's rules and regulations really didn't bother Steve too much. Actually, nothing bothered Steve too much. Fresh from Woodstock, his credo was live and let live or, better, love and let love. He didn't seem to be a typical Landry player.

In 1970, Steve Kiner was a hippie, but make no mistake, he could make plays! He was cat-quick and very instinctive. If he could conform, he had the potential to be a great player. So he made the team as a rookie that year.

The Cowboys' practice field at Forest and Abrams in Northeast Dallas was really just a vacant lot with a framed metal building housing the dressing and meeting rooms. The field was manicured perfectly, though, and the building's parking facilities were more than adequate.

Just as there were rules on the field and in the locker room, there were also rules to follow when in the parking area. The only reserved spot at the entire facility was the one immediately adjacent to the front door. That spot had a large sign attached to the wall that boldly stated: "HEAD COACH TOM LANDRY." Though that was the only marked rule in the parking lot, other rules were clearly understood. For instance, the balance of the spots along the front wall adjacent to Coach Landry's slot were reserved for the other coaches. There were no signs—the players just knew. The other unwritten rule was that the veterans always got the closer spots to the entrance in the remainder of the lot. The rookies got what was left—the last row and thus the longest walk. It doesn't sound like much of a perk, but throughout the NFL, there is a pecking order.

I arrived at the practice facility early on Thursday morning. It was pouring rain, so I had planned for delays, but made good time despite the storm. I parked on the "Rookie Row" at the back of the parking lot and rushed into the building with my coat over my head. By the time I got to the door, I was soaked. It was one of those Texas-sized storms—a gully washer.

I was relaxing at my locker when Steve Kiner arrived and immediately sank down into his locker. He flopped on top of his pile of shoes, propped his feet over the bench in front of his locker and pulled his baseball cap down over his eyes in an effort to catch up on some lost sleep before the 9 a.m.

meeting. I assumed one of his girlfriends must have dropped him off, because he was conspicuously dry.

Players continued to filter in, totally drenched and soaked to the bone. Though they were complaining about the weather, their spirits were high, as there was a glimmer of hope that practice might be cancelled. The locker room was loud, but it didn't disturb Steve. He was sound asleep.

It was approaching 9 a.m., when suddenly the decibel level dropped to an eerie low. I stood up to investigate the reason for the silence. It was easy to spot. The entire locker room had their eyes fixed on the totally drenched Tom Landry as he made his way to Steve Kiner's locker. Usually impeccably attired and always dapper, Tom Landry looked like a mix between a drowned rat and one of those street people who solicit money at the traffic lights. He positioned himself squarely in front of Kiner's locker as Steve lay snoozing under his cap. As water rolled off of Coach Landry's drenched hat, he reached up and removed it from his head. He then wiped his face with a handkerchief in his free hand, still holding his hat full of water. He proceeded to dump the captured water onto the slumbering clump and startled Steve to consciousness. Hungover, we could see Ft. Worth in Steve's drooping road-map eyes.

"Steve Kiner…man, you are something!" exclaimed Coach Landry.

"Thanks, Coach," Steve acknowledged The Man, unaware of any problem.

"That is your van in my parking spot, right?"

Steve nodded.

"What were you thinking?"

"Coach, my mama taught me to get out of the rain, and I know you're big on rules and stuff—but when it's raining that hard, there just are no rules!"

Steve Kiner did not get any special punishment that afternoon, but he didn't last long in Dallas.

"The Look"

We all thought coach Tom Landry's main passion in his life was definitely football. He told us, though, that it came third. Above all came God, then family, then came football. He really meant it. To him football was much more than just guys banging their heads together—it was an art form. He was a perfectionist, and he wanted his players to think and feel the way he did about football. He was very serious about the game and took extreme pride in his work. He demanded that his players do the same.

TL expected his players to fit his definition of a professional. That is, someone who sets high standards, is serious about his performance, and is proud of the results. Coach picked players who fit his style of motivation. We had Vince Lombardi quotes all over the locker room that supported this philosophy. For example: "The quality of a man's life is in direct proportion to his commitment to excellence."

Coach Landry had an uncanny ability to surround himself with players and coaches who were self-motivated and eager to please him.

He learned his coaching technique as a student of the great Vince Lombardi. Landry and Lombardi coached together under Jim Lee Howell for the New York Giants. That, along with his personality, made for a powerful combination. He had a very calm disposition and appeared to be in control of his emotions at all times. He never yelled or screamed to motivate; he analyzed, dissected, and directed.

When we came in at halftime, Landry never raised his voice. He first would sit and visit with the offense. He would diagram some new offensive plays that would attack the opponent's defenses or change certain blocking assignments that would do the same. Coach then would come and speak to the defense. If our opponents were putting points up, he would speak to us first. That was never good. That meant we weren't playing very well. He would generally tell us what we were doing wrong and then draw it up on the chalkboard. He would always go right to the heart of our problem and tell us how to solve it. We knew that if we could pull off what he drew up, we could stop their offense. Now that is motivation.

When we performed poorly on the field, he wouldn't yell, either. But he would give you a certain look of complete disdain—better known as "The Look." You did not want to get The Look, because that meant you were responsible for a major mess-up. Coach Landry did not mind physical mistakes as much, but mental mistakes always earned The Look. I only got The Look a few times in my career. If you were pierced by The Look too many times, you would not be around long enough to see any more looks.

One of those times was on a cold and windy afternoon in Chicago. The score was Chicago 21, Dallas 17. It was

The Look. ***Photo courtesy of Cowboys Weekly***

the fourth quarter. A field goal would not help us, and Roger and the offense were sputtering. Watching the video highlights of any particular season, one would never imagine a less-than-productive Dallas offense ever existed. In the perspective presented by the big Cowboy PR machine, the offense never faltered. On this day, although the offense was not performing, the defense was playing very well. We had stopped the Bears around their own 20-yard line and forced them to punt. There was about 1:30 left in the game, and I was the lone man back to return the punt. TL called me over to the sidelines from my safety position and started giving me instructions. He told me, "Cliff, fair-catch the punt. Got it?" He always said, "Got it?" to reinforce what he had just told you. Of course I said, "Yes!"

I had all intentions of fair-catching the ball. But it was a low punt—the best kind to return! The ball had a low trajectory and was falling short; some quick math told me the ball would get to me before the punt coverage guys could. So, several thoughts went through my mind as the ball was in the air. First, I knew that "The Man" told me to fair-catch it, and that was a big deal. But on second thought, I reasoned that I had been in the league long enough to know how to make the right decisions. I knew what to do and what not to do to win. My job at free safety was to take calculated risks…and not make mistakes. I decided to risk it!

So I caught the ball near our 40-yard line. No fair catch! "I'm going to pick up a quick and easy 10 yards at least," I thought. "Our offense is struggling. I might break the game open. The punt is low." Then I expanded those thoughts, "Maybe I can gain 20 yards, then run out of bounds, or maybe break it all the way if I can get a little blocking. But I have to stay next to the sideline so I can easily run out of bounds to stop the clock for Coach."

Things went just as I had planned. I gained the first 10 yards easily. Then I got greedy. Only ten more, I thought. I only had to juke one guy, so I cut back inside for a few yards before heading back to the sideline to run out of bounds and stop the clock—no problem. But as I was heading for the sideline, a guy hit me from behind and knocked the ball loose. It fell out of my hands and we both went down. The Bears player who hit me was lying on my legs, holding me to the ground. The ball was only a yard from my hands. I was clawing the AstroTurf of Soldier Field digging towards the ball. But one of the Bears fell on it before I could recover it. Damn! We were right next to our sideline. Coach Landry was standing five short yards away. I was frozen flat on the ground, with the guy still on my legs, looking up into Coach's face. He simply shook his head and gave me—you guessed it—The Look.

CHARLIE'S TALE

Samson

All of us who experienced the '70s had to deal with hair. Hair—and lots of it—was in. A rock opera, entitled *Hair*, had a successful run on Broadway. Hair was everywhere. No shaved heads, buzzes, or even close-cut haircuts. Hair on your head, facial hair, and sideburns were all ways of showing your social awareness. Cliff was known for his muttonchop sideburns and stylish Fu-Manchu mustache. I just let my hair go and grow.

One off-season after I had settled into my role as the strong safety, I was committed to becoming the strongest man on the team, pound for pound. That was my goal—never miss a workout and work out twice a day whenever possible.

One day, Coach Landry called me into his office for a "consultation." I questioned the nature of the visit even as I settled into the chair in front of his desk. I remember reflecting that I was glad I had shaved off that 10-day beard. "Charles," he said (I knew it was serious when he called me Charles), "I've seen your workout record, and I just want to encourage you to continue disciplining yourself to accomplish your goals."

I was shocked. Usually a personal visit with The Man resulted in a reprimand or warning. That was not the case, though, in this meeting. I was even *more* shocked when the coach then volunteered that he would no longer judge people by the way they looked. It was almost like a confessional. He expounded that cultural trends, like long-hair fads, don't change the hearts of people, and that I was a great example of that. He saw how dedicated I was in spite of my long hair.

Wow, what a relief! I stood up, made eye contact with those serious, cobalt eyes and shook his hand saying, "Thanks." I would be able to work without worry.

On Friday afternoon, three days later, I swung by the practice field to catch my second workout of the day. Not concerned about grooming issues, I had not shaved since my visit with Coach Landry, nor did I bother to "style" my hair after my morning shower. I entered the building, walked down the hall towards our locker room and took a sharp right around the corner, when I bumped into Coach. He had just showered and had a towel cinched around his waist.

"Charles!" I knew I had startled him with my sunglasses, three-day beard, cowboy hat, and wild hair. "Gosh, Charles, when are you going to get a haircut?"

"What?" I was stunned and confused. I took a step back, pulled my sunglasses off and tried to gather myself. I guess he saw the confusion in my eyes and he attempted to make a joke (TL didn't joke much). To assure me that he remembered his newfound philosophy of acceptance, he made this analogy: "I know, you can't cut your hair because you're afraid you might lose your strength...like Samson!"

I started to enjoy this exchange now, because clearly the coach sensed my fear of still being judged by my looks rather than my production. In the spirit of that moment of humor and also to let him know that I recognized his Samson comment as an apology, I jabbed a little joke back his way. "Yeah, Coach...Samson. We all know about Samson. Look at you; you lost your hair and when you did, your leg went gimpy." (Coach Landry was bald and had a bum knee.)

He responded with a chilling look, and the joking was abruptly over. He gathered his composure and methodically responded, "The functionality of my left knee is not directly proportional to the loss of my hair." Then he turned and limped away.

Habits are slow to change.

The Impossible Takes a Little Longer

Coach Landry was a strategic genius. He would have made an excellent field general during a time of war. He

An engineer by education, our coach knew the enemy better than they knew themselves. ***Photo courtesy of Cowboys Weekly***

designed both the Cowboys' complex offensive system and the formidable Flex defense, which dominated opponents' offenses during the Doomsday era of America's Team. He also pioneered the use of computer analysis in football. Because of this, he knew what was happening on both sides of the ball. By the next game, he knew our opponent inside and out.

During the season, Coach Landry spent time in both the defensive and offensive meetings. He generally spent more time with the offense but would come in, usually on Thursday, explain our defensive strategy, then relate it to our game plan for the upcoming Sunday. He always defined the three main objectives that we needed to achieve to win the game. Sometimes those objectives involved certain plays, for example: "Stop the Vikings' outside running game." Or they could focus on an individual, like: "Control Chuck Foreman and keep him under 100 yards." We had confidence that, if we could execute the plan he set out, we would win. We then broke up into individual groups and discussed how we would execute our part of his plan.

Sometimes during the year he would design new blitzes for a particular offense. In one of our playoff games against the Vikings, he designed a new blitz. He saw something on a film or in our computer analysis that inspired his creativity. It was designed especially for their "Brown" formation. On a Brown formation, the fullback lines up behind the QB, and the halfback lines up behind the tackle. Typically, it is a running formation. Sometimes, though, play action passes were run with both backs moving to the weak side on a fake run move, then a pass developed.

When asked if he had ever seen Coach Landry smile, Walt Garrison answered. "Well, no... but I've only played for him for nine years." ***Photo courtesy of David Woo Photography***

A blitz is typically designed to send two of our three linebackers after the quarterback at the same time. With only one linebacker left to cover two backs, it forces the free safety to cover the remaining back. For added pressure, Landry's blitz of the week against the Vikes sent all three linebackers in a never-before-run "triple blitz."

In his own confident and inspiring way, Landry was going through and defining everyone's responsibilities. "First," he said, "D.D. Lewis, our Wanda linebacker, is blitzing, and on the weak side, Cliff covers the halfback. Then on the strong side, Thomas Henderson, our strong-side linebacker, is blitzing, and Cliff is covering the fullback."

What?! Wait a minute! I was supposed to cover both backs at the same time? Surely he had made one of his few mistakes! I couldn't cover both backs at the same time!

It is not an easy task for a free safety to not give a blitz away. You must line up 10 yards deep, away from the potential receiver, usually the halfback, and still cover him. If the quarterback reads the blitz and quickly dishes it off to the halfback, you need to be right on him. If you are a few yards off, you've really got your hands full trying to catch a quick halfback with a lot of field in front of him and everyone else upfield blitzing—no help in sight.

Under normal circumstances, covering two guys is virtually impossible. On a Brown formation, though, both Landry and I knew the chances were remote that both guys would come out at the same time. It did give me a chance to see how Coach Landry would answer my question, though.

I mentioned to Coach Landry that I knew he had confidence in me, but did he know he had me covering both backs at the same time? He said firmly that he knew and that both backs would not come out at the same time. I hesitated and then said, “But, Coach, what if they do both come out at the same time?”

Again, he said they wouldn’t.

“But just what if they did?”

“They won’t.”

“But just in case they do, what should I do?”

“Just cover the one they throw the ball to!”

In the later part of the game that Sunday, the Vikes came out in a Brown formation. We called the Triple Blitz. I was nervous as hell. The ball was snapped, and just as our computer printouts predicted, a play-action pass developed. Sure enough, they only sent one back out. I covered him and we sacked the quarterback.

Of course!

CHAPTER 4

Cowboy Legends

CHARLIE'S TALE

Spike

The 14th week of the 1979 season brought the New York Giants into Dallas. I had to sit out that season, since I ended my 119-game streak with an ACL tear in a preseason game with the Seahawks. I dropped by the practice field during the week, and I remember Drew Pearson, our number-one clutch receiver, bragging to me in a teasing way that he had gone 100 straight battles without missing one because of an injury. That's quite an accomplishment for a wide receiver.

Drew had an uncanny feel for going across the middle. Roger's favorite receiver, it seemed like whenever we really needed a first down, Mr. Clutch would come through, usually on a crossing route between the linebackers and the defensive backs—dangerous territory.

It was a feat to enter enemy grounds like he did so often and never get hurt. He got hit, but he was so tough, athletic

Agile and athletic, Drew Pearson turned clutch catches into TDs. ***Photo courtesy of Cowboys Weekly***

and smart that he would get up unscathed and return to the huddle.

Drew always played his best games against New York. He was raised in New Jersey, and it inspired him to reach deeper, plus he loved competing against Terry Jackson, the New York corner who had Drew's number.

He was determined to have a great game. And he did, but his consecutive-game, injury-free streak came to an end that day. It was a crossing route in the kill zone that did Mr. Clutch in, but it wasn't the bloodthirsty linebackers or defensive backs who delivered the blow.

Drew came in motion across the backfield, but Roger ended his cadence prematurely and the ball was snapped before Drew cleared the tight end. Drew managed to weave his way through the maze of players reacting to a run fake. He cleared the first level of defenders, and with his built-in radar, he set off on a path through the land mines that would keep him clear of shots from the bad guys.

As Drew read the coverage, he was able to accurately see who was responsible for him: Terry Jackson. His route was so creative and imaginative that he spun Jackson completely around and created just enough space between them for Roger to zip a pass to him. Drew caught the perfect pass in stride, quickly dodged a linebacker, juked the safety, and outran Terry Jackson to the corner of the end zone.

He and the Dallas faithful were elated. I watched from the sidelines as Drew celebrated his success by leaping into the air just as the official threw his hands up to signal the touchdown. While in the air, Drew was torn between spiking the ball at Jackson's feet and heaving the ball into the stands.

His indecision resulted in neither the spike nor the throw, but a combination of both. When he lost his concentration, it appeared he lost all coordination also. When Drew came down he bore no resemblance to a professional athlete. An unbalanced, awkward landing caused his left leg to hyperextend. He went limp for a second, and then his pride took over. No way was he going to let the fans and the Giants know he had injured himself executing an end-zone celebration.

He kept it to himself for the rest of the game, but he had injured himself, and badly. Not badly enough for surgery, but badly enough to miss the next two games. The diagnosis: a severely sprained knee. This athletic, smooth, controlled and smart future Hall of Famer was a victim of the end-zone celebration.

We all knew Coach Tom Landry despised end-zone acts, but not because of a chance of injury. It was because he was from a generation that rarely brought attention to themselves and never humiliated a opponent. The excitable expressions after touchdowns did both.

Drew played the next series with his sprained knee. He swears Coach knew his showboating had hurt him. Drew thought that because Tom Landry abhorred end zone celebrations, he had called Drew's number just for spite on the first play in the next series. Amazingly, Drew ran another great route and hauled in yet another touchdown—all on his bum knee.

Contemplating the irony of it all, Drew realized his performance string had been broken. Mr. Clutch was stuck with a new nickname that served as a glaring humble reminder of his spastic episode. Teammates take no prisoners.

The greatest clutch receiver in Cowboy history was, from then on, known as "Spike."

CLIFF'S TALE

Snoozin'

Every day during the season we started our meetings at 9 a.m. If you were late, you were fined. The fine doubled on each occurrence, starting at $50. Generally, guys weren't late. The whole team met first with Coach Landry. After Coach told us what it would take to beat our upcoming opponent, the defensive team would break away into our own room. Defensive coordinator Ernie Stautner met with us all together, then we would separate again: defensive backs with Gene Stallings, D-line with Ern, and linebackers with Jerry Tubbs.

Ernie is a Hall of Fame former Pittsburgh Steeler. He was definitely from the old school. When he played, they did not use facemasks—you could tell by his nose that it had been broken several times. He played at a time when there were no "prima donnas" and it was a man's game. No artificial anything—no AstroTurf—only grass and mud. It was blood and guts. There were no such penalties as "unnecessary roughness" or "unsportsmanlike conduct" then. No one wanted to mess with Ern. That toughness filtered to all of the players he coached.

In each of the rooms there were eight-millimeter projectors for viewing the films of our practices, games, and the upcoming week's opponent. The projectors had very hot bulbs. That heat, combined with the monotonous whirr of the machine, made staying awake difficult at times. It was even more difficult if Ernie was going over the D-line play on the goal line. The goal-line defense for the linemen was either in or out, but it took 45 minutes to explain. If you weren't involved, you might find yourself in la-la land. That is, until Ernie or Gene would ask a question about what your responsibility was on a certain offensive set. Your teammates would laugh if you were caught snoozing or stuttered out an answer.

An imposing figure for QBs, 15-year veteran Jethro Pugh made our jobs easier. ***Photo courtesy of the Dallas Cowboys***

It never fazed Thomas Henderson. Our talented but uninvolved linebacker kept his head on the desktop. He was seldom awake in meetings and never knew what the defenses were or even who we were playing most of the time. Tubbs tried to keep him awake, to no avail, and generally just wound up letting him sleep. Charlie would fill him in on what to do during the games.

One time when the whole defense was together, Ernie was going through a long-winded analysis of a short-yardage play. The projector was whirring away, the room was stuffy and the lights were out while we watched some team run a short-yardage dive play over and over. All of a sudden in the middle of Ern's dissertation, the room was illuminated. The lights came on and washed the film out. Everyone started looking around trying to figure out what was happening. We finally spotted the culprit.

Jethro Pugh, our big defensive tackle, had fallen asleep. He was so tall that when his head fell backwards it hit the light switch and turned the lights on. The only problem was that it did not wake Jethro up! He was snoring away as everyone was dying laughing. Someone finally poked him. His eyes opened wide as if he had seen a ghost. Many of us were rolling on the floor by then. Of course, Jethro had to run a little more than the rest of us after practice to make sure he would sleep that night.

Cool Hollywood

Tom Landry used film sessions as a great coaching tool. He would critique every player at the point of attack. No

Talented and athletic, Thomas "Hollywood" Henderson was laced with potential...but undisciplined.
Photo courtesy of Cowboys Weekly

one was immune to his criticism. Coach Landry demanded complete attention from every player. Even those players who were backups could not relax during a Landry film session because they, too, could be brought to task.

Thomas "Hollywood" Henderson was cast from a different mold. He certainly had his own drummer's beat, and he was laced with talent. Plus, Tom Landry didn't intimidate him. No one did, for that matter. He was so athletic, strong, and bright that pro football came easy to him. He was full of confidence. Thomas also had an engaging personality. He could charm the fangs off a snake and he had an infectious smile. He was a mess, but he was a treat to play with.

Once, when Tom Landry was critiquing Sunday's game film and then turned to discover Thomas leaning against the wall with dark sunglasses on, he was aghast. Thomas really pushed Coach Landry to his limits.

We were all squirming in our seats when The Man slowly stood up and sauntered over to the light switch. Thomas was oblivious to everything. No telling what he was dreaming about when Coach Landry flipped the lights on and addressed Hollywood, "Thomas!"

He paused for Thomas to regain consciousness. "Can you explain why you have sunglasses on in the dark?" Coach Landry asked.

Thomas flashed his most charming smile as he sat up. With no intention of removing his sunglasses, he welcomed the challenge with his response. "Coach," pausing for effect, "when you are cool, the sun's always shining on you!"

Tight-lipped, Tom Landry just shook his head.

CHARLIE'S TALE

Randy White "The Manster"

Randy White was the best pure football player I was ever exposed to. He was completely committed to the game. Randy's body was so tuned for functional strength that even his love handles were as hard as bricks. He wasn't like most men or much like most football players, for that matter. So concentrated on perfection was he that he manufactured a

Randy White (part man, part monster) was impossible to escape when the enemy was locked in his crosshairs.
Photo courtesy of Cowboys Weekly

war machine of himself. Although he was very knowledgeable about football, he was somewhat naïve about other subjects. Randy's charming, innocent demeanor transformed on game day to this despicable, nasty, destructive...well, "monster."

From this unique combination of split personalities I spawned the nickname "The Manster"—part man, part monster, but perfect football player. He scared me on game days, but entertained me on all the others. He was one of those guys whom you were just thankful was on your side when the fight started.

Horse Pills

One Friday after practice, Randy reported to the training room requesting something for his upset stomach and constipation. Don Cochran (Cocky), our trainer, after handing Randy two oversized suppositories, said, "This will fix you right up. Do both of these before you go to bed tonight, and you'll be like a new man, er, monster tomorrow."

Randy accepted Cocky's medicine with relief and a bit of apprehension when he saw their size. He cut his eyes toward me as he held the pills and sort of chuckled. The next morning I was in the whirlpool when I observed Randy reporting to the trainers. He obviously felt better because he had regained that bounce in his step and that twinkle in his eye. Cocky quizzed him, "How do you feel, big fella?"

"Great! You were right, those horse pills did the trick, but gosh, they tasted like @#$%!"

Game Face

The Manster was all monster on game day. During competition, his personality was frightening. Not only did Randy never help an opponent up after he knocked them down, he didn't even help his teammates up. He scared me while in the huddle, so I just never talked to him. He had a wild, hateful look in his eye. I guess it was all part of whipping his opponent not only physically, but mentally as well. The only time I blatantly disobeyed Coach Landry's orders was when, while meeting him on the sideline during a timeout, he demanded that I go out to the defensive huddle and rip Randy for not getting enough pressure on the quarterback. So when I did report back to the huddle with the defensive call, I looked at Randy, lost my nerve, and said, "Keep up the good work."

Kung Fu Master

But Greg Kouch, a journeyman offensive lineman, did break the code on Randy. I think Greg was the only NFL player who enjoyed playing against Randy White. Certainly he was in the minority. Greg was a solid NFL player, but showed his intelligence by returning to law school after his playing days. He obviously didn't take the game quite as seriously as Randy. It was truly just a game to Greg Kouch. To Randy…it was life. Greg's wit always kept Randy off balance.

To witness, at one game the NFL program, *Gameday*, featured the All-Pro "Manster" on the cover getting martial arts instruction from Dan Inosanto, Bruce Lee's student.

What a great feature—the perfect football machine was attempting to be more perfect by incorporating Eastern hand-to-hand combat into his arsenal. During the game, a post-whistle tussle occurred within my earshot. Two massive dinosaur types were clashing into each other, with the officials attempting an ill-advised separation. They butted and collided so hard one time that they repelled one another, creating a distance between. Greg Kouch and Randy White squared off again, and I distanced myself. Randy, fresh from his "Jeet Kune Do" martial arts lesson, struck his ready-to-fight pose.

Greg, seeing that, dropped his mitts, opened his palms with a questioning gesture and asked in a teasing octave, "What are ya gonna do, Manster...Kung Fuuuuu me?" The Manster was tamed that day and burst out laughing. Greg Kouch got Randy out of character. Randy hated that he liked Greg—in an entertaining way.

Manhole

Randy met him on the field one more time before Greg went off to law school. Randy was determined that this time Greg was not going to get him out of character. Besides, he had an image to maintain. Halfway through the third quarter, it was a similar scene: two Titans plowing into each other after a play had been blown dead.

When they broke from each other this time, Greg, openly irritated at something Randy had done, announced, "Your nickname is wrong. You are not a Manster—part man, part monster. You are a Manhole—part man, part asshole."

Greg's silliness triggered Randy's sense of humor again. His image tarnished, Randy was glad when Greg Kouch retired.

CLIFF'S TALE

Pain...or Injury?

Pain is a part of everyday life in pro football. During the season, every morning it hurts to get out of bed. Your body takes a real beating. The burning desire to perform on Sundays is an addiction that pushes you through the pain. You learn to shut pain out of your mind. Watching a game on TV does not give you an accurate portrait of the true intensity. When you see a devastating hit on the TV screen, you think, "Wow! That was a good hit." In reality, if a normal person were hit that way he would be hospitalized or even killed. The reasons the pros can get up afterwards are because they are young and incredibly fit, they are truly tough, and they know how to "take a hit." And sometimes they are a little crazy!

Even then, at times, professionals have to be carried or wheeled off the field. This can be very serious, and in a lot of cases, it not only puts you out of that day's game, but can also cause debilitating long-term effects. Injuries often affect the outcome of the game. They are just a part of life as a pro football player.

There are many sayings associated with pain in football. One of the most common is: "You have to learn the difference between pain and injury." That is a coach's way of saying suck it up and play.

There are several levels of toughness within the player ranks. There are players who will play with broken bones and those who will stay out with a sprained pinkie. All those who play through the pain are tough, but some are tougher than others.

The effects of injuries knocked both Charlie and me out of games more than once, but we learned to play with pain throughout our careers. Not only did we learn to block out the pain, we blocked it out so that we could play with as little distraction as possible.

There were several ways to help come back from an injury. The training room on Monday after a Sunday game was always full of recovering victims.

The basic treatment was "contrast," and that old standby has been a part of football for decades. There was a giant tub filled with hot water—the old whirlpool. Next to the roaring tin tub was a 50-gallon plastic tub filled with ice and water. Injured players would hold their legs or arms or whatever hurt in the very hot whirlpool water for a few minutes and then dip it into the ice water in the tub for the same amount of time. Man, that is a test of mettle when you have a pulled hamstring high on your leg and have to stand in freezing cold water. Contrast therapy theoretically opens and closes the blood vessels and starts the blood flowing through the injured area, thus speeding up the healing process.

We had all the newest high-tech medical equipment. There were always players getting treatment, with devices attached to their bodies. The main goal was to shorten injury time and to get them back on the field as soon as possible. Besides the whirlpool, there were ultrasound, heat packs, a neck-stretching device to separate smashed neck vertebrae, and more. We even had an acupuncturist come in and stick us full of needles.

The next level of treatment was a bit more serious—Dr. Knight, our "horse doctor." Dr. Marvin Knight was old school—a brilliant doctor with a rough exterior. He was a crotchety, old guy with a dry (sometimes even sadistic) sense of humor. He lived in a little town north of Dallas on the Red River called Muenster, Texas. He drove down weekly to treat the team and fly with us on our away games. He understood the coach's definition of the difference between hurt and injury, and most of the time he would say, "You are not injured. Get your ass back out there!"

I will always be indebted to Dr. Knight. He saved my career one year. In a preseason game in Oakland, I hurt my knee. Marvin did not travel with us to that game, and when I hobbled off the field, the doctor who checked my knee said I had torn a ligament and that it needed to be operated on. The next day, the Cowboys flew me back to Dallas and drove me up to Muenster to see Marvin. He checked my leg and said, "Hell, your ligament is only stretched. We are going to put it in a cast. You will play in a few weeks." He then said, "Son, your knee is not going to put you out of football. Your neck is!" And he was right.

Marvin had cures for the common, everyday football injuries that would have debilitated most people. If you weren't getting back to full speed fast enough in the tub, Marvin had another route. The fastest way back into the game was the "shot"—a cortisone shot combined with a little Novocain right on the spot that hurt. It more or less "lubricated" and, at the same time, numbed the injury so you could hit the field again. I had many of these shots throughout the years in my shoulders, ankles, and knees. They did get me back on the field quicker, but there is no telling the effect they might have on me in the future.

Of all the shots I received, the most painful was in the arch of my foot. The injury was similar to "turf toe," but in my arch. It was caused by extreme pressure on the arch when pushing off hard to cut or break. The trainers told me it was an incomplete tear of my plantar fascia, and to heal it needed to be completely ripped away from the bone. To make it tear the rest of the way, they told me to push off very hard and it would finish the job. The only problem was that every time I pushed off, a jolt of pain, like a knife, jabbed into my arch. The pain shot from my foot all the way up to my head. I think I have a high pain threshold, but that was like no other pain! No matter how hard I tried and how much pain I endured, I could not make it tear.

The other option was a shot right on the spot—the most tender part of my foot. Marvin laughed and said, "Cliff, this is going to hurt you more than me!" He had never said anything like that before, so I readied myself for some real pain.

Whoa! When he stuck the needle in, I really thought I was going to pass out. It took my breath away. It felt like 50,000 volts of electricity jolting through my body. The shot may have helped, but there was no way I would ever do that again.

Your body, not your mind, tells you when it is time to retire from professional football. That injury happened later in my career, and while my body was compensating for the arch injury, I pulled the hamstring on the other leg.

When I began spending more time in the training room than on the practice field, I knew my body was signaling time to quit. We all played with different levels of pain, constant and otherwise, and with different injuries, but going out on Sundays and performing was worth the price of playing.

CHARLIE'S TALE

Uncluttered Mind

Clint Longley was a true character. His two favorite things were snakes and guns. Having gone to school in West Texas at Abilene Christian College, Clint had been exposed to the Texas rattlesnake. He had two as pets and brought them to training camp. Understandably, by choice, his room was off limits to a good many on our team.

After he made the team his rookie year, he asked one Friday after practice if he could drop by my house on a Saturday before a Sunday home game. My house was on three acres, two miles from the practice field. I encouraged everyone to drop by.

I was in the front yard that Saturday afternoon when Clint drove up in a 1957 Cadillac—a low rider with huge tail fins. The back seat had been completely removed and Clint had a pony in the back where the seat had been. The pony's neck and head stuck out one window and his tail stuck out the other. His mane and tail was flying in the wind as Clint drove up.

Clint jumped from his car, in cowboy boots and a hat and asked, "Can my pony stay in your back yard?"

Only Clint.

Against the Redskins, one-day wonder Clint Longley performed a miracle on Thanksgiving. ***Photo courtesy of Cowboys Weekly***

I couldn't accommodate the pony, because our backyard fence had some problem areas, so we found a spot with one of our neighbors.

That year Clint only played in one game, but, boy, was that ever a big game. It was Thanksgiving Day, and Dallas was hosting the evil Redskins. It was during the height of the Cowboys/Redskins rivalry. Their "over-the-hill gang" announced before the game that they were going to rough Roger up and knock him out of the game.

Early in the third quarter, they did just that. Their 13-point lead would surely hold up, and they were giddy with joy. The Washington team didn't even know who our backup quarterback was, but by the end of the game they had figured it out.

All Clint did was engineer two touchdown drives, one on the first series he was in and the other in the fourth quarter with 45 seconds left to beat the Redskins. He would swagger up to the line like a gunslinger, drop back and fire. Completion after completion followed. The 'Skins didn't know how to defend against him.

Both touchdown drives were capped with two long touchdown passes, one to Billy Joe Dupree and the other to Drew Pearson, over the heads of the Redskins' secondary. I guess they didn't think he could throw the ball very far, but he did that day.

Blain Nye, Stanford's All-Pro guard, summed it up best after the game: "We just witnessed the triumph of the uncluttered mind."

Racing Roger Staubach

Training camp in Thousand Oaks wore us out. Every day seemed to be the same—a beautiful, sunny, 90-degree summer day in Southern California. Every morning, we woke up to the clanging of the chain from the flagpole outside the dorm.

The ritual was to pull our sore and beaten bodies out of bed in time to walk through the California Lutheran College campus to the cafeteria for breakfast, put some fuel in our stomachs for the morning practice, and then walk to the locker room. We were fined if we did not make it to breakfast before a certain time. I was always sore, and it was hard to walk because my feet hurt. They were under a great deal of stress from running and cutting every day during practice. There were young guys hobbling as if they were old men on the path to the CLC open-air cafeteria. No one talked very much. We just sat down, ate, and then left to get taped for the morning's practice.

The training room was always lively, however. The trainers were chattering and complaining because they had been bent over taping ankles and knees all morning. The early risers were telling jokes and laughing. I wasn't in the mood. It was too early for me. After we were taped, we stiffly pulled our shoulder pads over our heads, struggled with our jerseys, and fumbled our shorts on. (We wore shorts in the morning and full pads in the afternoon.) Then we took off up the dusty trail to the practice field.

Outside the locker room, there were always tons of kids asking for autographs that they probably lost before the afternoon practice. They walked with us, carrying our helmets. When we reached the field, we started our warmups. Before each practice, we had to run two warmup laps around the quarter-mile track. It was a real pain and every step hurt, because one, we were running in cleats that were meant for

Roger Staubach, commander of America's Team, was the most competitive and productive QB of our era.
Photo courtesy of Cowboys Weekly

grass, not a track, and two, we were always beaten up, stiff and sore…unless we were a QB!

In the mornings, Roger Staubach was always chipper and ready to go. He would go out early to throw to receivers, and I would go out to practice catching punts. Roger is one of the most competitive guys I know. He loved to compete in anything. He is a winner, and in the fourth quarter, the defense knew that if we could stop our opponents and get the ball into Rog's hands, we could win. There were times, though, that I did not want to compete with him.

Sometimes we would walk together up the trail to practice. I generally tried to avoid Roger in the morning, because he always wanted to race me on the last part of the warmup lap. I didn't want to race, because I was stiff and he wasn't. I also knew that I would have to run my tail off during practice, and all Roger was going to do was throw passes or hand off to a running back. Of course, Gene Stallings made us run, cover, tackle, and hit all practice long to get us in shape.

Our race always started the same. First, I would tell Roger I didn't want to walk with him because I knew that he would want to race. Then he would tell me that he was not going to race today. I knew it was a lie, but I would reluctantly agree to walk, and therefore jog, with him anyway. We would start out slowly around the track on our first lap, and then, with about 220 yards left on the second lap, Roger would try to edge just a little ahead of me. I knew what he was doing, and I would pick my tempo up equally to stay even with him. He would start sprinting to try to get ahead of me, and I wouldn't let him. Finally, like madmen, we would sprint the last 100 yards.

After our race, while we were trying to catch our breath, Roger would laugh. I knew I should have conserved my energy for practice, but it was a fun daily ritual. Of course, I could not let him beat me, so I never coasted. I also never learned, and we went through the same process day after day through training camp.

CHARLIE'S TALE

Ambushed

I witnessed the most disturbing event in my career in the Cowboy locker room during Clint Longley's second year. During training camp, Clint had visions of more playing time because of his performance against the Redskins the year before. He had only played one game since Roger recovered and finished the season. Clint was stuck on the bench the whole year, and that disappointment festered in him.

In a passing drill during one morning practice, Clint took a verbal shot at Drew Pearson for running a route poorly. Roger corrected Clint, stating that Drew was in fact right in the way he ran the route. Clint shot a wise comment back at Roger, and an argument ensued. Before it escalated on the field, Roger kept his cool and suggested that they "solve it after practice."

No one on the team knew that they had had words, so when we heard the screams "Fight! Fight!" later, we had no idea it was the quarterbacks. Linebackers fight, but not quarterbacks. Practice was over and most of us were lifting weights. We all dropped what we were doing and sprinted to the baseball field, where there was a mountain of dust.

In the middle of the dust, Roger was on his knees, pummeling away with Clint under him. By the time we got to the pile, Roger had established dominance. It didn't look like Clint was hurt, but he did get the worst of it.

Coach Landry called us all together and reminded everyone, "This stuff happens, it's just the nature of football. Any ill feelings need to be left on the field and not carried forward. It's over." Or so he thought.

After we showered, we were all in a festive mood because of the rare quarterback fight. We were all proud of Roger for being such a man's man. He was a true leader, one who is not afraid to fight if the cause is important enough.

Then we sauntered up to the dining hall for lunch, looking forward to an afternoon nap. When I got my tray I noticed Clint sitting alone, so I joined him. I recognize that there are two sides to every story/argument, so I really didn't hold it against Clint for scrapping. Actually, I understood. Like Coach Landry said, that stuff happens. Especially when jobs are on the line.

We small-talked through lunch. I noticed a scrape under his left eye. He got up and took his tray, got some ice cream and rejoined me. Then he announced, "I know how I can get traded!"

Clint had requested a trade in the off-season since he knew who the quarterback for Dallas was and would be for a long while—and it wasn't him. He wanted a chance to start.

"How?" I questioned his declaration.

"You'll see." He got up and left.

The midday break flew by. The nap was too short and afternoon practice came way too soon. The mood was subdued in the locker room for the afternoon practice. People were still groggy from their naps, plus everyone was sore from the morning. The decibel level went up the closer it got to report time. I walked over to the scales and weighed, then logged my weight in the "before practice" column. When I stepped off the scales, I saw Roger putting his shoulder pads on.

It's an awkward thing to negotiate; those pads are so cumbersome. When he had both arms through the shoulder harness and popped his head through the middle, Clint Longley cold-cocked Roger with a right cross.

I could hear an uncomfortable crunching sound and then Roger's head snapped back and hit the wall. Both impacts did damage, and Roger slumped to the ground, dazed and confused.

Randy White grabbed Clint, so we didn't have to worry about him anymore. Several of us helped Roger up. It wasn't pretty. The more Roger regained his wits, the madder he got. Randy held Clint at bay and we manhandled Roger to the training room. He was fiercely trying to get to Clint.

Our trainers took over and attended to Roger's needs. I rushed back to the locker room. Randy still had Clint with one arm clamped around his waist. Clint was wildly animated, but he was going nowhere. While Randy held Clint under his arm, it looked like he was hauling a sack of feed. Since Roger was with the trainers in the training room, we let Clint go. He immediately sprinted up to his room, grabbed his bags, which were already packed, and drove down to Los Angeles to catch an afternoon flight to Dallas.

It was a good thing that Clint left, because after the doctor sewed up Roger's cut, cleaned the wound and cleared him for practice, instead of heading straight to the practice field, Roger beelined it to Clint's room. When he crawled through Clint's dorm window, he found an empty room, except for his rattlesnakes. Roger wanted to do some damage, but wisely he stayed clear of those snakes.

I cannot fathom how mad Roger had to be.

Clint Longley was traded the next day.

We never saw Clint again. To Roger Staubach's credit, he never retaliated. A true test of character, he abstained from getting even. His fiery personality won't allow him to talk about it, even today. He's been haunted all these years knowing how much he'd like to even the score, but always setting a good example, Roger was "above it."

When reporters dug and found out that he had streaked back up to the dorm, they probed and questioned Roger's Christian standards by asking him just what would he have done if he had found Clint in that dorm room, Roger's response was, "I'd have turned the other cheek."

CHARLIE'S TALE

Looney Tubes

After the first eight years in the NFL, your body switches from steady maturation and improvement to the opposite—deterioration and eventually demise.

Training during the off-season was to strengthen areas of your body to perform your specific job description at your position. Later in the season, it was more for maintenance. Most areas of the body could be developed, but it is widely known that speed is not an area you can improve as you get up in years.

Our Eastern-influenced, Ph.D.-in-biomechanics strength and conditioning guru Dr. Bob Ward had other ideas. His theory was that the only reason you couldn't run as fast as you could as a rookie was because your body (and mind) had forgotten what it was like.

His solution was that if we could get our bodies and minds to experience the speed improvement, then we would have a better chance to actually run faster. It was a form of psycho-cybernetics, but rather than just dreaming of running faster, we would actually run faster—with assistance. Running downhill was one way to go faster; another was to run in a wind tunnel with the wind at your back. In Texas, we had neither hills nor a wind tunnel, but we had imagination.

Bob's initiative was contagious. He was so passionate about his studies that I started believing him. His uninhibited imagination came up with a simple way I could experience running faster—the slingshot effect. Bob showed up at practice one morning with two huge strands of heavy-duty surgical tubing, about two inches in diameter. One end of each strand was connected to a two-foot-square leather pouch; the other ends were loose.

Physical fitness guru Dr. Bob Ward.
Photo courtesy of Dr. Bob Ward

Dr. Ward summoned Cliff and me over to the goal post in the end zone and instructed us to tie the loose ends of the tubing around the back of the goal post.

"Be sure it's snug and tight," he instructed.

After those loose ends were secure, Bob ordered me to grab the other end and settle the pouch against my backside. He stood at the goal line with his stopwatch and asked Cliff to help me back up

40 yards. Cliff and I couldn't tell how long the tubing was, but we knew it wasn't 40 yards. When the slack was out of the tubing, we had stretched it all of 25 yards. From then on, each step back was harder and harder. I made eye contact with the doctor, looking for relief, and he just waved me back. By the time we got close to 40 yards, it took all that Cliff and I had to keep from stumbling forward. That tubing was stretched tighter than guitar strings.

Cliff held on tight to the leather seat. His feet were posted in the ground at a severe angle for stability. I arranged my feet in a starter's stance, and when I did that, Cliff could hold on no longer.

"GO!" he yelled to me, hoping Bob was ready. Bob started his stopwatch, and the tube's tension launched me five yards into the air before my right foot hit the ground. Soon my left foot followed and then my right again. Left, right, left, right, left, right. My legs were churning as I frantically tried to stay upright.

Bob had wanted me to experience the speed, and that was happening. I was flying! It was all I could do to keep up with my feet. The only thought I had during my lift-off was, "Gosh, I'll never remember how fast my legs need to go!"

With 15 yards to go, the G-force had relaxed a bit, so I could now open my eyes. When I did, all I saw was the goal post, which was what the other ends of the tubing were tied to. It was coming on fast. With no time to spare, I dove forward head first, hoping that the friction from the ground and grass would slow my pace and minimize the collision.

When I came to a stop, the top of my head was lightly touching the goal post. I heard Cliff scream between laughing fits as he sprinted up to me. He and Dr. Bob Ward entered my field of vision simultaneously. When I looked up there was not only grass, but roots and dirt lodged in my mouth, teeth, and nose, as I had body-plowed face first the last seven yards. Most of the tubing that had pulled me was now bundled up on top of me.

Dr. Ward proudly displayed the stopwatch and announced, "3.2 seconds. Awesome!"

CLIFF'S TALE

Warning Light

From my high school days on into the pros, I was told that I practiced unusually hard. To me, that meant that I tried to make the most out of practice and make it as game-like as possible. I know I worked hard, but I may have practiced with more intensity than most. It was nothing that I planned or did intentionally; it was just the way I was. I, unlike many, enjoyed practice.

I enjoyed the daily competition and preparation for the upcoming game. I tried to visualize myself actually playing in the game. Mental imagery and visualization were a part of my preparation to play. I may have hit my buddies in practice harder than I realized at the time. They either told me afterwards or I have heard them talk to others about how I hit them in practice. I am sometimes surprised.

There were times that I did want to send a message to the guys who were letting up in practice. From an early age it had been drilled into my head that if practice was like game conditions, the better prepared you would be for game time. It proved true, so I tried to get that message across to my slower-paced teammates. I wanted them to be mentally ready for the roughness in the game. I did not want to hurt anyone in practice; I was just trying to get their attention. I did not like to see guys loafing and would let them know—gently, of course.

During practice, as defensive backs, most of my and Charlie's interaction was with the wide receivers and quarterbacks with whom we were matched. We were either in man-to-man individual coverage practice, skeleton drills with just the wide receivers and quarterbacks, or total team drills, all of which involved the QB throwing and the receiver catching. We would, from time to time, get a shot at the running backs, but only in the team-oriented drills.

During my era with the Cowboys, we were blessed with some of the best receivers who have ever played, starting with Bob Hayes, the Olympic 100-meter champion, who was named "The World's Fastest Human." What an incredible title! With his speed, the game changed from primarily man-to-man defenses to zones to cover his fast, deep routes. There is no question that he should be in the NFL Hall of Fame!

There were also other great receivers, like Tony Hill from California and Drew Pearson from Tulsa. Drew was Roger Staubach's favorite target in the clutch. Drew and Tony really came through and made many spectacular game-winning catches, most times with only seconds left on the clock. Drew was on the catching end of one of the most famous plays in football history—the "Hail Mary" pass thrown by Rog in our playoff game against the Vikings.

Butch Johnson, Lance Rentzel, and Golden Richards were also excellent receivers, known as the best in the

Flashy Golden Richards had great speed, and potential to match. ***Photo courtesy of Cowboys Weekly***

NFL when they played. I had good relationships with our receiving corps and even felt sometimes as if I were their older brother. It was a "tough love" kind of thing. I helped them, but I would also jolt them in practice from time to time, just to keep them on their toes and let them know to never slack up.

I remember it happened once in an afternoon practice skeleton drill.

Golden Richards was a good-looking guy; the girls all loved him. He was a Utah boy with blazing speed. He started at the University of Utah, but finished at the University of Hawaii. He was nicknamed "The Blond Flash" because of his speed and long blond locks. He was running an inside route that day, and to me, it did not look as if he were trying very hard and was running his route at about half-speed. To let him know that that was not acceptable and that he needed to pick up the pace, I came up and popped him as Rog's pass touched his hands. I hit him a little harder than I meant to and knocked him out cold. The trainers ran onto the field and stuck ammonia under his nose. He opened his eyes and asked what happened. They told him, "Cliff hit you!"

The next day he had a surprise for me. Sitting in my locker was a bright yellow helmet with a flashing red light and siren on top. He gave it to me and told me he wanted to know where I was at all times! I thought it was funny. I told him not to let down in practice and he wouldn't have to worry about where I was.

The next day, all the guys dared me to wear the beacon hat in practice. They suggested that a little levity might be good for morale...if Coach Landry approved. Fat chance! A rookie would have been run off for wearing a silly hat like that to a Landry work session. I had been playing for Landry for several years and therefore had some credibility with the coaches. I might pull it off, I thought.

I was always serious in practice, and needless to say, so was Coach Landry. He wouldn't have it any other way. As a matter of fact, he was very serious all the time about everything. Even though he told us "the practice begins with the warmup laps, so buckle your chinstraps when you run them," I decided to wear it anyway. Not for the whole practice, but on the two warmup laps. "He might not even be there," I rationalized...and hoped.

Feeling unusually adventurous, I took the dare. I put the helmet on, turned the red flashing light and siren on and took off. I started trotting the warmup lap around the outside border of our practice field.

Whew! Coach Landry was not out there yet. I wanted to finish before he came out. Most everyone had seen and heard the hat. In the middle of my second lap, though, he appeared, coming out of the training room and onto the field. He began to walk toward where I was running. He stopped and stood at the goal post just as I was rounding the corner. All the guys were laughing. I did not see Coach until I turned the corner. Man, I was nervous. I was treading on thin ice! He turned his head only slightly, in typical Landry fashion, and grimaced. Boy, did I get "The Look" then. I don't think he thought it was a bit funny!

Of course, to make up for those antics, we had to win the game on Sunday and I had to play especially well!

CHARLIE'S ★ TALE

The Next Butkus

The only mistake the Dallas braintrust made with Randy White's career was that they didn't start him full-time until his third year in the league. Their thinking: He is another Dick Butkus. Though a lineman his whole college career, the Cowboys tried to make Randy White into a middle linebacker. He was fast enough, strong enough, and smart enough...he just had no experience at standing up. Plus, I don't want to accuse Randy of being shy, but let's just say he avoided attention. He had spent his whole college career keeping it simple, whipping the guy in front of him.

During my 12 years in the NFL, there were only three players added to our team whom I considered "different"—something that physically separated them from us normal athletes.

Those three Cowboys were Tony Dorsett, Thomas Henderson, and Randy White. They all had unlimited potential. Tony was fast through the hole and could shift to a gear designed for raw speed that we had never seen before. He was a phenom. Thomas Henderson resembled an animal more than a human. Gazelle-like, Thomas, too, had another gear. He could leap, spring, change directions, and flat-out run faster than any linebacker (and some wide receivers) I had ever seen. Plus, he was smart, strong, and mean. He had the most potential of all. Too bad it was squandered. Randy White certainly did not squander his potential. The Manster was never going to take a chance on not being able to live his dream, which was to be a Hall of Fame player.

His experience at middle linebacker can be summed up in one tale. Striving to work Randy in slowly, Tom Landry decided he would replace the great Lee Roy Jordan on third-and-short situations. Randy's mass would serve him well in this down-and-distance situation. Offenses at that down were semi-predictable—mostly simple power plays designed to pick up the first. It seemed like a perfect opportunity to get his feet wet at that foreign position.

We were at Veterans Stadium, and it was the first series in our first game against the Eagles. On third and one, the Eagles changed personnel to suit the situation. They went with the "Jumbo" package, and the big backs were in. Dallas, likewise, utilized situational strategy. Middle linebacker Lee Roy Jordan at 212 pounds was replaced by massive, 270-pound Randy White.

The middle linebacker was in charge of the huddle. The middle linebacker and strong safety made calls and change-ups as an extension of the coach on the field. After receiving the call from the sidelines, the middle linebacker would step up into the huddle, make the call and sometimes give a coaching pointer or a reminder and then break the huddle. A typical call would be: "Short yardage, Flex weak blitz, red dog verses all movement. Ready…break!" In rhythm we would all break with a synchronous clap, then move to our positions, just like any football player, on any level.

When Randy arrived at our huddle that first time, the gap reserved for him was nearly closed shut. No problem for Randy, though, as he nudged himself inside, forcing the linemen to make room. He now was the center of attention, a role Randy was unfamiliar with.

All eyes and ears in the huddle were trained on our leader—the middle linebacker. The average years of experience (excluding Randy) in that huddle were well over eight NFL seasons, and we were all waiting on our short-yardage call from someone who had never started one NFL game.

As I scanned the huddle, I cut my eyes over to Randy. I saw a man out of his element. The pregnant pause created some classic brook-trout looks from our team.

Randy successfully barked the short-yardage calls in practice, but this was different. He had his hands propped on his knees, but his head was down, avoiding eye contact from anyone. That's when I sensed something was seriously wrong. The leader should not have his head down. It's up, looking his teammates in their eyes, speaking with authority and conviction, and exuding confidence that your call is the right one for what's ahead.

Those looking at Randy for direction found nothing but rivers of sweat pouring out from underneath his helmet.

He never looked up. Finally, as the Eagles were breaking their huddle, he panicked and blurted, "Ready…break!" clapping his hands in an attempt to break the huddle. That's the only thing he said—no call, no alerts, nothing, just "Ready…break." To his credit, he did say that with conviction. Randy was overcome with a sense of urgency to get off the stage. Breaking the huddle got him out of being the center of attention, so forget the call.

Our team had no instructions.

There was a brief moment of chaos, until Cliff and I calmed our veteran group by audibling a short-yardage defense that would work against all formations. Doomsday settled into the correct alignment and stood poised to attack, just as the Eagles got set. Even though the cat had gotten his tongue, Randy did look ominous at the middle linebacker position.

The power play off right tackle was short of the first down as Randy and company stuffed the ball carrier at the point of attack for no gain.

That was Randy's last play at the middle linebacker position.

CHARLIE'S TALE

Toni Fritsch "I Keeka the Touchdown"

When the NFL abandoned the conventional straight-on style of kicking and discovered the soccer-style kicker, the Dallas Cowboys searched for the best. Vice president of personnel development Gil Brandt took his kicking guru, Ben Agajanian, and some scouts on a kicking caravan to Europe, the hotbed for soccer.

For six weeks they traveled throughout the soccer kingdom in search of the next Jan Stenerud. They gambled on an aging Austrian ex-superstar named Toni Fritsch. Toni had passed his prime on the national soccer team, but there was possibly a future for him kicking an odd-shaped ball in American football. We never knew how old Toni was, but we heard that he had played for the Austrian national team since he was 16.

When he arrived in the United States, Toni was balding and a bit out of shape, especially by soccer standards. He couldn't have been more than 5'2" tall. He looked like an

Easter egg with a helmet on top and feet on the bottom—but could he ever kick!

Toni could not speak one word of English, but he never felt any pressure, having played in front of kings and queens and hundreds of thousands of soccer fans. I was the holder for 10 years with the Cowboys, so I was very close with the kickers. Toni once volunteered to me after he learned broken English that when he was introduced at games, the entire throng of soccer crazies would chant "Toonni! Toonni! Toonni!" According to Toni, he was a national hero. I never doubted it, based on how well he could kick.

The first game Toni appeared in was in St. Louis, at old Busch Stadium. As was the norm for our games with the "Cardiac Cardinals," the game boiled down to the final two minutes. With the game tied and only 10 seconds left on the clock, the Cowboys lined up to kick the winning field goal from 43 yards out. Toni waddled onto the field, with the single-bar facemask not protecting his face, but appearing to be an extension of his chin.

The Cardinals called time out in an attempt to"ice" our kicker. With World Cup experience, Toni couldn't be iced, even if he had known what icing was. When play resumed and we lined up, I remember the Cardinals' great free safety Larry Wilson screaming at Toni, "Hey, Kraut, you're gonna choke!"

Too bad Toni didn't understand a word of English. Snap, hold, and kick. Perfect!

"No problem!" Toni proclaimed as we carried him off the field.

The headlines in *The Dallas Morning News* featured a classic quote from Toni: "I keeka the touchdown."

"Me...Dallas Cowboy"

When Toni first arrived in Thousand Oaks, California, we all felt sorry for him. He knew no one and could speak no English, and all he did was watch cartoons on television all day...in English. But, boy, could he kick! One day he got his interpreter to bet Walt Garrison that he could not only make every field goal he kicked by splitting the vertical uprights, but that he could land the football on the horizontal crossbar on every kick. After 12 kicks, starting at 20 yards and moving back to 48 yards, Toni had successfully landed the ball on the crossbar of the goal post on all 12. Incredible! My confidence went up with regard to Toni's accuracy after that display, and he collected $100 from Walt.

Walt got him back, though, that night. When the 11:00 curfew rolled around, the troops were still hungry. Walt conned Toni into sneaking out, driving to town and picking up a pizza for us. He told him that kickers don't have curfews because they don't work hard. Another enticement was that Walt was treating on the pizza, and Toni loved pizza.

Toni sneaked out of the dorm, drove three miles into town, picked up the pizza, and was hurrying back to campus a little too fast. The Thousand Oaks police spotted him speeding and pulled him over. He got out of the car, he had no license, and he spoke no English, but he told the police, "Me," pointing to his Dallas Cowboy-issue T-shirt, "me, Dallas Cowboy."

"Sure you are, buddy, and I'm the Lone Ranger. You are going to jail!" the police replied.

Luckily, Gil Brandt pulled some strings that night and got him released. Our pizza arrived a little cold, but Walt felt as though he had gotten even.

"Lean It a Leetle Bit Back"

Toni held off all contenders for his kicking job with the Dallas Cowboys for seven years. In his eighth year, Coach Landry was pressing for a new kicker because Toni's range had shortened. Tom Landry had been a punter in high school and college, so he felt qualified to critique and coach the kickers. I know Tom Landry's presence evoked a pressure that was equivalent to what was felt on game day. He stood five yards behind the spot of the kick. These kickers were under more pressure than imaginable because Tom Landry also had a cameraman film every kick at ground level so he could analyze the differences in the kickers.

I'm glad I was just the holder and not the kicker. Being the holder, I did everything I could to make the competition fair, striving to make perfect holds for every kicker. Of course, each kicker had his preference on the vertical position and the lean of the ball. For instance, Toni loved his leaned back and tilted towards me a smidgen. All kickers had the seams of the ball facing the kick direction. The snap, hold, and kick all took place in 1.3 seconds. It was precise.

Tom Landry made a crucial announcement at the team meeting one night that would affect all of those competing for the kicking job. He wanted all of the kickers to have the exact same hold, eliminating all variables. That should have been great for me, because all four kickers in the running for the job had different preferences. Coach Landry wanted the ball perfectly vertical (not leaned back or tilted).

Coach Landry had read some physics study that said it would be aerodynamically advantageous if the ball were kicked while in this upright posture. The new policy was fine by me, but all kickers are individuals, and they are borderline weird about their preferences on holds. Thus the crux of my problem: Tom Landry's hold standardization, instead of making my job easier, complicated the matter.

At the next afternoon practice, Coach Landry was watching every kick from five yards back with his stopwatch in hand, and a prone cameraman was filming every snap, hold, and kick. Every phase of the kicking game was recorded, filmed, and analyzed by Tom Landry. After warming up at 20 yards, we moved the entire drill gradually back. The vertical holds were not affecting the kicks one way or the other as far as I could see.

When we positioned our kicks at 48 yards out, though, things changed. The first three kickers in the competition struggled with the vertical hold at this testy distance and failed to make the kicks. Then it was Toni's turn.

Kickers have the exact same routine before every kick—actually before they do anything—because they are so superstitious. The procedure to line up a kick is always exactly the same. First, the holder gets the spot exactly seven yards, two feet behind the center and places his index finger on the ground at that spot so the kicker can get his bearings. (Some kickers even go as far as changing the position because a blade of grass might be too long.) Next, they go straight back two yards and over two yards, take one last look at the goal post and re-establish concentration on that spot. Then he nods to the holder that he's ready. The holder acknowledges the nod, whips his head into focus on the center and holds his free hand up so the center has a target for the snap. The snap fires back, the holder snags the ball, places it on the spot (usually tilted or leaning), spins the laces forward and frees his second hand just in time for the kick to explode through the ball—all in approximately 1.27 to 1.32 seconds.

It was Toni's turn now, after the three others had missed their tries at 48 yards. He addressed the spot with his right foot pawing at the ground like he was scratching for gold. He then bent over and pretended to look at his target, the goal post. He was so short, that when he leaned over, his helmet almost touched mine as I knelt. I placed my left hand down, confirming the spot he had chosen.

I then glanced up to get eye contact with Toni. With Tom Landry in earshot, Toni, ventriloquist-style, spoke out of the side of his mouth, with his head and helmet pointing forward, and whispered a desperate plea, "Lean it a leetle bit back, please, Chally."

"What?" I asked with my eyes, appalled that he would outwardly defy Coach Landry's decree.

Then he repeated pleadingly, not making eye contact with me, just body bent, head forward, mouth contorted to the side, "Lean it a leetle bit back, please, Chally."

"Oh, this is nice," I thought, "Put me in a predicament, why don't you?"

Toni took his two steps back and two steps over. We made eye contact and he nodded. I received the snap, placed

Toni was a true pro, but in his uniform he looked like an Easter egg. ***Photo courtesy of Cowboys Weekly***

the ball on the spot and…leaned it a little bit back as Toni requested.

He drilled the kick.

The next day during the film session I knew Coach would bring me to task, but he never said a thing. Surely he had spotted my leaning hold. I guess he had his favorites, too.

Toni hung onto his job.

CHAPTER 5

NFL Superstars

CHARLIE'S TALE

Sweetness

In 2002, Emmitt Smith broke the all-time NFL rushing record previously held by Cliff's and my good friend, Walter Payton, "Sweetness."

"Sweetness" was the nickname he gave himself, and it fit very well. His running style was, well, sweet. He was quick, powerful, and imaginative.

We got to know him in the Pro Bowls that we all played in for the NFC. I had heard he was a special person, and after meeting him, it was verified. He loved the game, and he loved to run and play. At those Pro Bowls, every day after we had finished practice, Walter would organize a wild touch football game. We'd stay and play touch football for an hour after practice, like a bunch of fraternity brothers home from college who get a yearning to play some "ball" after Thanksgiving dinner.

My first game-situation encounter with Sweetness came in 1975, my inaugural year at strong safety. I knew that he

Walter Payton was a class act, even when he was leaving our guys (like Larry Cole) in the dust. ***Photo by AP/WWP***

had a burst and that he could cut on a dime, so I knew he was good. I just didn't know how good...until we played the Bears.

They broke their huddle and set up at the line of scrimmage in a split formation. Our scouting report screamed end-run sweep, and that's what came. Both guards pulled, and the fullback cut the outside linebacker. Walter took the hand-off and swung across the backfield, following his lead blockers.

I focused on the interference and engaged the lead guard. By the time I had played off his block, Walter was on me. I remember thinking: "He's not so good. I've got him."

But thinking I had him was as close as I was going to get. Under control, I waited until it was a can't-miss tackle, one that I could deliver a blow with.

As Walter attempted to turn the corner, I cut him off and then exploded into him. Problem was, he wasn't there. Like Houdini, he disappeared. I got nothing but air as I fell harmlessly face first into the Texas Stadium turf. I looked up in time to catch his number 34 running the other way. He had stopped, dipped, spun, and changed direction in a flash. He now was reversing his field.

"%#*&!" I screamed and scrambled to my feet, madder than a hornet. I don't miss tackles.

I kept him in view as he circled back behind the line of scrimmage. By now he was on the other side of the field ready to turn the corner.

I projected where he should be by the time I traversed the field. I set my sights to "cut him off at the pass." I decided I would blindside him this time since he wouldn't see me coming. As I streaked across the field, I noticed all the would-be tacklers who lay in his wake.

I picked up speed as I honed in on Sweetness. He was so busy juking another Cowboy, he never saw me coming. I had him in my crosshairs, and I pulled the trigger. I coiled and exploded with that 34 clearly in view. Then it was gone. I flew through the air yet again, only to land face first on the turf yet again. This time I was totally embarrassed.

Only Walter Payton could make me look so bad. Frequently, I would go four or five games with no missed tackles. Incredibly, I had missed him twice on the same play. How sweet it is.

CLIFF'S TALE

Billy's Rough Night Out

The legal violence on the football field demands a complete commitment to intensity and ferociousness. Throughout my career, I found it was easier to not know my opponents. It was easier to think they were the villains or bad guys, even when maybe they weren't. Today, and even later in my career, many of my opponents became my good friends. At that time, though, I did not want to let up on anyone. It was just harder to really smash and try to obliterate someone I knew. Meeting and getting to know my opponents—even befriending some of them—complicated my life in the football arena. I wanted to keep it simple. I did not want to like them. Therefore, I tried not to know or get too close to the folks across the line from me.

Sometimes Charlie would try to motivate me by fueling my anger during our pregame routines. He would tell me, "Man, can you believe that Mel Gray is such a prima donna? He is cocky and thinks he's gonna blow by you."

"No way!" I would respond, pretending to allow him to tune me up for the inevitable confrontations with the nasty and also dangerously speedy Gray.

In my early years, before I went to any Pro Bowls, I did not know any players in the league, and they all were targets. I had no mercy for anyone. After playing in a few Pro

Bowls and spending time with some of the top players in the conference, I would sometimes drop my guard and even say "Hello" before some games.

That was the case with the Washington Redskins' quarterback, Billy Kilmer. Billy was a real winner. He was the kind of quarterback who would "draw plays up in the dirt" and beat you. In his early years, he was a triple threat. Before the pros he was an excellent player for the UCLA Bruins. When I faced him on the field in the latter part of his career he was competing more from his heart than with his athletic abilities. But he was still dangerous and could beat you. Billy was the kind of guy whom I would naturally like under different circumstances.

Playing the Redskins in RFK was Charlie's and my favorite game of the year. It always seemed to be a critical game in the outcome of our season. We both would be very prepared and totally fired up for the game. The Skins/ Cowboy rivalry during my era was intense, and the teams and fans hated each other because we were usually vying for the divisional crown.

Our team styles completely contrasted. The Skins were a group of tested and tough older veterans led by the scrappy Kilmer. The Cowboys were depicted as the clean-cut, "All-American" players led by Captain America, Roger Staubach, who navigated the sophisticated Landry ship. With the contrast came a deep rivalry and an intense dislike. Both teams, though, were loaded with talent and sent several players to the Hall of Fame.

The Redskins had a speedy receiving corps led by Hall of Famer Charley Taylor. Charley was the toughest receiver I

Gritty competitor Billy Kilmer didn't win with style points...he just won! ***Photo courtesy of the Dallas Cowboys***

faced in my career. He was a converted running back traded from the Cleveland Browns. He wore me out!

In one particular game in our not-too-rambunctious Texas stadium, however, I thought we had the edge. It was one of those games that would move one of us into first place in the division and closer to the Super Bowl. That day there was more enthusiasm than normal, and we could feel the electricity in the crowd. They understood the importance of that game.

But the reason we had the edge had little to do with our players or our game performance. The Thursday night before our Sunday afternoon game, Kilmer was relaxing and had hit a few bars on the way home from George Allen's practice. Billy had one too many brews and was pulled over by the Washington police. Reportedly, they gave Billy a DWI. Of course, that made the headlines in all the Washington papers: "Kilmer DWI before the Cowboy game."

The fun had just begun, because Ernie Stautner, our defensive coordinator, with T.L.'s approval, had put my favorite play in the defensive plan—a safety blitz. All right! It was my chance to blast up the middle of the line and split right between the center and the guard, knocking the stuffing out of Kilmer, just as he was setting up for a pass.

But Billy was a seasoned veteran and a savvy QB. He could smell a safety blitz and would deliberately change his cadence to throw off the safety, who was anticipating and timing his dash through the sweat hogs.

Well, the play was called, and I thought I had timed it just right to slip by the hogs and blast Kilmer for a loss and more humiliation. He instinctively paused in his cadence and caught me redhanded at the line of scrimmage, so I slammed on my brakes to keep from being caught offsides. At the moment the ball was to be snapped, the action screeched to a halt. I was off balance, leaning over the line of scrimmage, standing face to face with Kilmer. He looked right at me and said, "Cliff, you've got to give me a break today. The Washington press is killing me with that DWI. Give me a break!"

Kilmer got me; I didn't know what to say or do. What he did wasn't fair or right! I wasn't supposed to like him or give him a break, but on that day, on that play, I had to find another way to compete. Kilmer was my buddy and still is today, but later in the game I did time my blitz right. I jolted him with all my might...then helped him up.

CHARLIE'S TALE *Tattooed*

Earl Campbell was a can't-miss senior recruit out of John Tyler High School in Tyler, Texas. The University of Texas rode Earl for four years, just like John Tyler did. He was a workhorse. So when he was drafted number one by the Houston Oilers in 1978, he was tagged a can't-miss pro, too.

Dallas always played Houston in our last preseason game for some unknown trophy called The Silver Boot. I never knew who created the trophy, nor did I ever see it, but I knew what the franchises were hoping for with this game: competition. The intrastate rivalry that seemed natural never materialized. It was because we rarely played Houston during the regular season. They were in a different conference.

The muggy August night when Houston traveled to Dallas, that can't-miss college star running back had a grand total of just 73 yards *combined* after all three of Houston's preseason games. He had been welcomed to the league. Watching him on film, it appeared that the phenom was really just another big back who was hesitant to hit the hole and quick to bounce outside—lacking the burst of speed needed to turn the corner—who maybe could be counted on for short yardage. Needless to say, he had not made a mark—yet.

The last preseason game was a tune-up for us and for Houston. It was more like a regular-season game in contrast to the usual characterization of most preseason games.

Both Cliff and I were scheduled to play three quarters, as were all of our starters. Earl Campbell had two carries in Houston's first series and had gained a predictable four yards. So far his performance was nothing special, just the same indecision and the appearance of the lack of raw speed.

The second series was a little different. The first play featured Campbell taking a hand-off from QB Pastorini, who reversed out from center. The left guard pulled to execute a perfect "quick trap" inside. All three blockers at the point of attack, both guards and the center, successfully fitted on their assigned men. Even the second line of defense, the linebackers, were shielded from making the play as I watched the blocking scheme develop to perfection. It was now time for Cliff and me to earn our money. The burden fell on us to replace those defenders, fill the hole, and hold the ball carrier to a short gain.

Part of the reason Cliff and I were All-Pro was because we played such a critical role in Dallas's stop-the-run Flex defense. Original NFL safeties were perceived as the last line of defense that played the pass first and last. Old-school safeties, vintage Paul Krause, weren't expected to be weapons against the run. Safeties were just that: safety valves. They had never been used as two extra linebackers, which was essentially what Cliff and I were. We had the toughness of undersized linebackers combined with the speed and agility to put equal emphasis on the pass coverage.

Several of Dallas's defensive schemes featured both of us, eight yards deep and ready to plug the holes at the line of scrimmage. Gone were the safeties who just made touchdown-saving tackles. Effectively, Dallas created a nine-man front when we were in the box.

So when Big Earl Campbell appeared in that tunnel created by his blockers, Cliff and I were ready to plug the hole. Cliff closed in on Earl's left side, and I on his right. We timed our charge perfectly, like we had done so many times before, so we would collide with the brute at about three yards past the line of scrimmage. By design we would explode at the exact same moment.

That was our signature—double-team 'em. Never make an apologetic tackle. We always made a statement when we hit the ball carrier, knocking them back...with prejudice. We had one fist of iron, the other of steel.

Earl had a low center of gravity. He had tree-trunk legs and a perfect leaning technique. The target appeared very ominous—tank-like—when we locked him into our sights. We crashed into him simultaneously. Immediately, we were both rejected.

He repelled our advance as he exploded into us. I flopped onto my butt, and in perfect sync, so did Cliff. Earl had an answer to our "statement."

As I lay on my back, I was amazed that after that blow, I still had my mental faculties. Lying there I saw and then felt Earl's size-12 cleat stomp down on my chest. He was churning like one of those massive earthmovers that acknowledge no obstacle. Certainly I had been no obstacle as I lay flat on my back pinned to the turf under his huge right foot. As he attempted to also crush Cliff, who lay nearby,

One lone tackler rarely brought punishing Earl Campbell to the turf. ***Photo courtesy of Cowboys Weekly***

Earl stumbled a bit, freeing me. I rolled over frantically and reached up to grab anything. His shirt tail was loose. I lunged for it and successfully clung to the tail of his jersey.

I held on with my left hand as the real big Earl finally cleared himself from pesky Cliff Harris. While escaping Cliff's initial effort, he mauled Cliff's thigh with his left foot just as he had collapsed my chest with his right. Cliff then rolled over onto his stomach and stretched with both hands and successfully clamped down on Earl's left ankle. He held on for dear life. We had him now…right?

After a 14-yard gain, he finally crumbled to the turf. He dragged us both, with no intentions of going down, until Bob Bruenig and D.D. Lewis leaped on his back. Four tacklers did him in.

Earl Campbell gained 223 yards that night against Dallas's vaunted Doomsday Defense. The way I felt the next morning, I could swear that 200 of those yards were right over the top of me. He had humbled our iron and steel into marshmallows and JELL-O.

That night, the NFL was introduced to Mr. Earl Campbell, rather than the other way around. It is unexplainable—the films I saw must have been another person. For my entire career, I never met a back who was as hard to bring down as the punishing Earl Campbell. He was, without any question, the most prolific workhorse-type back in the history of the NFL. I have five cleat-mark tattoos to prove it.

THE Tight End

In each position in football there are certain personality types. Jackie Smith personified the tight end position. Generally they are tough guys with bad attitudes—free-sprit types. He was a really tough, fast receiver who would not tolerate intimidation from anyone. The tight end position is a unique blend—the speed and catching ability of a wide receiver, the blocking ability of an offensive lineman and the mental toughness of a linebacker. Jackie Smith was the best tight end I ever faced.

In analyzing opponents, I always wanted to know everything I could about them, including what drove them.

Jackie Smith's size, speed, and strength, combined with his toughness defined the tight end position.
Photo courtesy of Cowboys Weekly

I began my analysis by knowing the basics: his size, speed, agility, quickness, and strength. Then I tried to understand, more subtly, a mental or emotional component. I wanted to know about a guy's mental toughness or find out if he had any emotional weakness. Some NFL players overlooked this component. Knowing how to get to a guy mentally sure made my job easier and gave me an edge. If I could make my opponent think about me and not his job, it detracted from his performance. It worked sometimes…on Jackie.

The Cardinals had the most potent offensive scheme in the league directed by head coach Don "Air" Coryell. They were loaded with offensive firepower. Led by the talented Jim Hart at QB and with one of the best-ever quick backs, Terry Metcalf, they built their foundation on speed. With lightning-quick outside receiver Mel Gray on one side, big-move guy J.V. Cain at the other side, and big, fast, wide receiver-type tight end Jackie, they had a perfect blend. Jackie was used as a deep threat who could open up defenses, and he was also a good blocker on running plays.

As an eager young defensive back trying to play mental games, I would mess around with Jackie. It was never anything serious, just enough to distract him. He did have a temper and would sometimes let it rule his actions. If he ran a turn-in route in front of me, and Jim Hart's pass was to someone else, I would sometimes come up from behind and pop Jackie in the back of the helmet with my forearm. It didn't hurt him much; it just rattled him a bit and made him really mad. Dave Edwards, our strong side linebacker that lined up over Jackie on every play, told me one time to lighten up on Jackie because he was taking his anger out on Dave. I laughed and knew my methods were working. Surely Jackie would drop a pass or two thinking about me.

In one game in St. Louis, I really made Jackie mad. He and I were jostling around after one play. I told him he wasn't really tough or something foolish like that. He said to me, "OK! Let's go!"

I said "OK!"

"Meet me in the parking lot after the game!"

"Are you kidding?" I asked. I wouldn't even think about meeting him outside the field without a helmet and pads.

We generally played our first Cards game in St. Louis, and then they would come to Dallas. Jackie and I had gotten into it a bit when we played in St. Louis, and it carried over when they came to Dallas. On one of the first series, the Cards had the ball and Jackie came downfield on a route. But instead of running the route, he came after me! When he got close enough, he hit me right in the stomach with his fist. The surprising hit knocked the breath out of me, and he laughed. An official flagged him immediately with a 15-yard personal foul. He told me he didn't care, that he was going to be after me all day. But that was just the result I wanted; my mental games worked again!

One time in St. Louis, though, the psych-out worked against me. It was right before halftime—third and 10 on about our 25-yard line. I had worked Jackie into a pretty good fury. The defense that was called isolated me on Jackie in a man-to-man coverage with no help from any linebackers or Charlie. It was a test—a defense we ran to throw Hart off and confuse him since I did not normally cover the tight end man to man. We hoped that in the time Hart took to analyze what was happening, we could trap him. Hart was not fooled. He saw me isolated on Jackie and threw the pass to him on a turn-in route.

As the ball was coming toward Jackie, I was in good position to knock it down. When it got there I could not reach completely around Jackie to knock it down because of his size. He caught the ball, and I tried to tackle him. He spun around with me holding on. He was heading for the goal line. My arms were around his waist, but when he spun he flung my body parallel to the ground. He threw me off with centrifugal force and took off. Several other guys and Charlie tried to tackle him next and missed. He not only made a first down, he went on to score.

I learned not to make him too mad!

The next year, I was headed for the training room on a Monday. I was going in to get treatment on my beat-up body. To get to the training room, I had to walk through a deserted locker room since everyone had the day off. Just the injured guys came in for treatment.

I will never forget what was waiting for me by the training room. I saw a big guy I did not immediately recognize sitting on one of the locker seats before the training room door. I thought he looked like Jackie Smith and that he was there to beat my tail. When he saw me, he stood up and walked toward me. I didn't know what to expect. He stuck out his hand and said, "Hello, Cliff. I'm Jackie Smith. I am your new teammate." Boy, was I happy to hear that!

With his intensity and winning ways, he immediately became a team leader and helped us get to the Super Bowl that year. We became great friends and still are to this day.

He has a giant photo of me being thrown off that day in St. Louis hanging in his office!

CHARLIE'S TALE

Cow-Poke

I hated playing the Raiders. I guess I was not alone in my feelings. They represented an element of fans and society that were on the dark side of gray. The Raiders looked mean—

and they were mean. The Raiders looked evil—and they were evil. The Raiders played outside of the rules and they paid for it, notoriously claiming each year to be the most penalized team in the NFL. But they won a lot of games and they did have a strong following, albeit a little skewed.

It was a blessing that the clean-cut, Boy Scout-imaged Dallas Cowboys, coached by the "white-hatted" Tom Landry, did not often play the nasty, gangster-type Oakland Raiders, managed by the "black-hatted" Al Davis.

I think that I hated playing them the most because their style always distracted us from our game. Which means they won a little victory every time we played because, I admit, the Raiders got us out of our game. Coach Landry's Christian principles were his guide. He always stressed to us the importance of keeping our poise, turning the other cheek and keeping our power under control. He wanted us to play our game.

The Raiders were masters at intimidation and distraction. Never did we play them when we didn't have a fight or, even better, a brawl. These brawls never resulted in injuries because of all the pads and armor we wore. With all of that protection we sort of felt invincible, but for some reason, when we played the Raiders, I feared I would pick a fight with the one player who had stuffed a switchblade in his pants or a chain under his shoulder pads.

We were in Oakland and were winning a close game. I had managed to avoid the first two fights in the game, but I was very perturbed, earlier having been a victim of two cheap shots after the whistle. I had avoided a confrontation, but I knew I was "losing it" and that the Raiders' plan was working:

Cliff Branch was small by NFL standards, but he could fly.
Photo courtesy of the Dallas Cowboys

they were distracting me and I couldn't get control of my emotions. Against my better judgment, I had to retaliate! So when I dropped to the middle zone position about four yards deep in the end zone on our pass coverage, I had my radar up, looking for enemy intruders. As I read the quarterback's eyes, I saw a silver-and-black blur in my peripheral vision entering my area.

I acted like I didn't see him, hoping for a surprise shot when he got in range. It was Cliff Branch. He was flying across the end zone on a route and would cross about a yard behind me. He didn't think I saw him, so I caught him by surprise as I turned, coiled and exploded with what I hoped would be a right forearm in his face, all in one motion.

How I missed my mark, I'll never know. But I did. Cliff Branch ducked my attack with the quickness of a hiccup, cursed me and continued on his route. I swear, the Raiders are trained for that stuff. They anticipated retaliation, even from the cool Cowboys. So they must work at it, they have to. I envisioned their training camp to be something resembling James Bond's 007 training site, complete with martial arts combatants sporting state-of-the-art weaponry.

The play ended with QB Jim Plunkett, under pressure, launching the ball harmlessly out of the back of the end zone.

I was a little embarrassed and ashamed of my actions as I strolled back to our huddle, only to be confronted by a madder-than-a-hornet Cliff Branch. He was pissed! Reflecting on the moment, I distinctly remember how little he was. I found myself looking down through my facemask at the top of his helmet.

"Gee," I thought, "if I am going to pick a fight with someone, at least it could be someone my size."

Size didn't matter, though, because the fight was over in a nanosecond. Branch got right in my face (by standing on his tiptoes), screamed some obscenities and then, as swift and efficient as Muhammad Ali's right lead, Cliff Branch drove his forefinger and his middle finger through the small opening between the crown of my helmet and the facemask and poked me in the eyes.

"Aagghhhh!!!" I screamed as my head snapped back. It felt like he had driven my eyeballs to the back of my head.

Blinded, I stumbled after the little worm, grabbed him and shoved him. The whistle blew and then the flags followed. I guess the official was alerted when I screamed like one of the Three Stooges and only saw my retaliatory shove. I was penalized for unsportsmanlike conduct—half the distance to the goal. The Raiders scored on the next play and we ultimately lost the game.

Kicks, cheap shots, bites, knives and chains. I can see those unconventional tactics being taught at the Raiders' camp, but pokes?

CHAPTER 6

Super Bowls

Ralph Neely's Super Bowl VI Accident

You would think after the intensity and brutality of playing a pro football game on Sunday, players would look forward to a nice, relaxing day off. Most players did. Some were recovering from injuries or soaking in the training room whirlpool. Relaxing at home was much too boring for us, though. There was a group of us who chose a different form of escape: dirt bikes! Suzukis, Yamahas, Husqvarnas meant to fly over the country trails. They were not street legal—no headlights or license plates. These bikes were designed just for riding in the dirt off the paved roads. They had big knobby tires and low gear ratios, but they could still travel extremely fast.

We had a lot of great times with those bikes. Of course the management did not approve of such recklessness. Coach Landry's theory was this: Do what you want in the off hours, but you better not do anything to embarrass the team or hurt yourself, or you will be replaced. He wanted us to act like professionals. Boy, if he only knew!

There were several of us who made up the "Pack." The whole diversion started with our tough and extreme strong- side linebacker, Dave "Fuzzy" Edwards. Dave loved dirt bikes and could ride like a pro. It was a fast and dangerous sport, and the danger became addictive to us. In time, Charlie and I became very skilled and even raced under assumed names in some motocross races. We were young and wild and rode our bikes way too fast. There were others who went along primarily for the camaraderie and the outing. They paced themselves. Walt Garrison, Dan Reeves and Mike Ditka were smarter. They had fun, but did not endanger their health. Charlie and I were invincible… we thought.

Some of the guys should have gone slower but didn't. Ralph Neely was one of those guys.

On one unusually warm and sunny Monday in January, we were at the very end of our season. The Pack had gathered at Lake Dallas. Our plan was to "release" stress by screaming around the trails that meandered at the edge of the lake. It was a fun place to wear yourself out on your day off. The trails wound up and around through the dry creek beds and curved through the scraggly oaks and thorny mesquite trees. There were steep hills to climb with sharp turns at the top you had to make so you did not go flying off into space. One of the goals of the ride was to not "eat dust." That meant the guys in the rear of the pack tried to race to the front to keep from breathing all of the dust and rocks kicked up by the riders in front.

Before the NFL/AFL merger, both leagues were competing for the talents of perennial All-Pro Ralph Neely.
Photo courtesy of Cowboys Weekly

Most of the guys' bikes were around 250cc. Charlie and I both had fast 360 Yamahas (that is another story). Fuzzy Edwards had a monster 400 that he handled extremely well. On this particular day, Ralph Neely showed up with a brand-new 450 Kawasaki. The bike was a beast—very powerful and very fast, but not designed for the casual rider. You really had to know what you were doing on that bike. Ralph did not.

Ralph didn't ride very much, but in an attempt to one-up everyone, he went out and bought the biggest and fastest bike on the market. He did not realize that there was much more to leading the pack than just the size and speed of the bike. The bikes performed only as well as the guys riding them. Your quickness, strength, and agility translated into high speeds through those narrow and curvy trails. Like returning kickoffs, you really had to be on your toes. If you were not, miscalculating was very dangerous, and running into trees at high speeds could kill you. Charlie and I had two friends who were killed by high speed misjudgments on dirt bikes.

That day, while we were racing around the lake, Ralph was constantly falling over and crashing. When he did we would stop and wait for him. He would get up and curse the bike and kick-start it, and we would all take off again.

After the long day of riding, we gathered where we had left our cars and trailers. We were all shot, just like we wanted to be on our day off—perfectly exhausted. Ralph looked over at me and said, "Cliff, come with me." So I did.

We took off and rode a few hundred yards to the backside of the spillway of the Lake Dallas dam. The spillway was a 300-yard-high grass covered hill. It was not too steep, but there were no trees. It was long, but not tough to make. Ralph said, "Let's take this hill." I agreed, took off first and maneuvered my way up the hill.

I was sitting on my bike, resting at the top when Ralph started up. When he had made it about halfway, he fell over. He cursed and coasted back down the hill. He backed away from the base about 150 yards and yelled to me, "I'm going to take it in second gear!"

I saw Ralph hammer down and really take off, blazing on his new 450cc monster. He whined his machine through first and shifted into second right before he reached the base of the hill. He was probably going 60 mph. He was really screaming up the hill.

"Wow!" I thought as he reached the top and went airborne. He flew by me six feet in the air, but he landed incorrectly. An experienced rider would have known to keep his feet on the pegs (where you rest your feet when you ride) so that when he landed, the bike would absorb the shock. Ralph did not know that and he extended his legs and tried to land on his feet. It did not work. Both he and his bike tumbled. His bike was still running, spinning in a circle with him lying flat on his back in the dust near it. When I ran over to see if he was OK, I saw one of his feet laying flat against the ground and the other pointing in a normal straight-up position. He had broken his ankle!

That happened, unfortunately for Ralph, two weeks before our trip to Super Bowl VI in New Orleans. He was a great player—an All-Pro—and we needed him. Of course, Ralph did not make the trip with a cast on his leg. Coach Landry called Tony Liscio, a former Cowboy who had retired and had not played at all that year. Tony played in Ralph's offensive tackle spot in the Super Bowl against the Dolphins, and we won. Not only did Tony take Ralph's position and his paycheck…but he also got Ralph's Super Bowl ring. So much for a fun day off, huh?

CHARLIE'S TALE

The Blooper Bowl Super Bowl V

Super Bowl V was a match between an upstart team and a seasoned franchise: the Dallas Cowboys versus the Baltimore Colts. Played in Miami, the game was riddled with turnovers and wild, controversial plays. We looked at it as a defensive gem and the controversial calls were just the ones that didn't go our way. Naturally.

Two weeks before, we had finally won the National Football Conference. There was great joy and relief stemming from that championship game. For some, the championship game against San Francisco finally knocked the monkey off our back (or throat, choking Dallas into not winning a championship). Beating San Francisco legitimized our franchise, and we were looking to sweep all the titles by winning the new-to-the-scene Super Bowl.

The "Doomsday Defense" was at its peak with Bob Lilly, Jethro Pugh, and George Andre anchoring the defensive line, and Chuck Howley, Lee Roy Jordan and Dave Edwards backing up the first level of defense, and the secondary was shored up with Hall of Fame corners Mel Renfro and Herb Adderly. I was the only rookie, playing safety next to the great Cornell Green. I was playing because our starter and star rookie, my buddy Cliff Harris, had been called to serve his time in a National Guard unit in Arkansas as the Vietnam War escalated. I can't imagine how hard it was for Cliff to be drilling in a defensive unit to defend our country rather than drilling to defend against the Baltimore Colts.

I filled in for him seven games into the season. During the next seven games I roamed the free safety position, playing on instincts because I had nothing else to depend on. I ended up leading the team in interceptions. I think it was because I played quarterback and wide receiver in college. It sure wasn't because I knew how to play that defensive position. A great pass rush also helped. Coach Landry always believed that to build a great defensive team, the front four men were the absolute best way to make it happen. At the end of the season, we had won seven games in a row and two in the playoffs. Our defense went 23 straight quarters without giving up a touchdown.

That Super Sunday, I played a huge role in arguably the biggest, most controversial play in Super Bowl history. On third and 10, Johnny Unitas dropped back and looked to his left. He set up and fired a high pass that looked like it was intended for Eddie Hinton in the curl zone about 10 yards downfield. The route had John Mackey clearing on the left side, hoping to pull coverage onto him. He was deep and drifting outside as the ball was released.

From the free safety position in that zone defense, my responsibility was the deepest inside receiver, so I trailed Mackey at a safe distance. I saw the ball being released, and I was amazed when Hinton leaped up and tipped the errant pass—it was so high. When he hit the ball he changed its flight path, so I calculated the new trajectory and adjusted my path to cut in front of Mackey.

I was poised for a pick as the pass drifted over a blur of blue jerseys. I positioned myself to catch the ball out in front of me so I could still be in full stride. I accelerated in front of Mackey and got set for the interception that never came. Miraculously, the ball's flight changed again, and my worst nightmare occurred. Rather than floating into my hands, the ball passed behind me and right to the surprised Mackey. The deepest receiver, my responsibility, caught the ball. He slowed, claimed it, and then lumbered 60 yards for a touchdown.

As I spun around and started pursuit, I was thinking about the rule then effective in the NFL that has since been changed: two offensive players cannot touch the ball in succession. I was sure that the last person to touch the ball before Mackey hauled it in was Hinton, so after Mackey crossed the goal line, I turned and vehemently protested to the nearest official. I looked like a cartoon character jumping up and down, shouting. Tom Landry's poise had not yet rubbed off on me.

We lost Super Bowl V. That play was one of many that made up the Blooper Bowl, as it is now remembered. The big play, deep to Mackey, was the only true touchdown drive our defense gave up. Baltimore couldn't put a sustained drive together, but still we lost on a Jim O'Brien field goal with seven seconds to go.

As it turns out, the deflected pass to Mackey was legal. Mel Renfro slightly grazed the ball after it had been deflected by Eddie Hinton and sent it right into Mackey's hands. Dallas television ran the play in slow motion, over and over, and the blue blur that I saw as I was about to catch the ball was Mel leaping and hitting it.

Bob Lilly was so frustrated that on the final play when the clock ran out he launched his helmet across the field.

It flew about 40 yards into the air and crashed into the artificial surface, and all of the pads and chinstrap broke free in a heap.

It was 11 years of frustration for Lilly, but for Cliff and me it was just the beginning of an eight-year span of five Super Bowls and ultimately two world championships. Never did I participate in a stranger play than that one, though.

CLIFF'S TALE

"Woulda, Coulda, Shoulda..."

Through the years, there are certain plays that stick out in your mind—you remember them forever. It seems generally, though, offensive guys remember only the great plays they made and very few of their errors. It is as if they have a catalogue in their minds and a detailed record of each of their shining moments. They get very specific with the down, distance, hash mark, score, whatever. They know every detail of their heroic deeds.

I think, as a rule, defensive guys are different. They remember some of their good plays, but more often they can tell you the plays they would like to do over. They remember the plays they want to go back and change—the plays they messed up on. They, like offensive players, have them recorded forever in their minds. I think it is simply because of the way defensive guys' brains work.

Defense is built around players reacting to a certain set of circumstances in a certain way. If that reaction means a poor performance or if they were beaten, then they store it away so as not to make that mistake again.

Naturally, if you have too many of these plays early in your career, you will have a very short career. You can't make a lot of mistakes and be kept around. Sometimes, though, you have to take calculated risks to make the big plays. Percentage-wise, you have to be ahead of the curve to take those kinds of chances. You have to play by the book early and build up enough points to take risks. The longer you are around, the more latitude you are given within the Landry system to be creative.

I can tell you, very vividly, which plays I would like to do over. Everyone makes mistakes in games and in life; remembering those mistakes helps make you a better player and a better person. But those are the kinds of plays that you lose sleep over.

One of those plays that I would like to change was in Super Bowl X in Miami. We were playing the Steelers. It was in the fourth quarter and we had stopped Bradshaw, Swann, and the high-powered Pittsburgh offense. We had them punting, backed up around their own 10-yard line. Bob Walden, their punter, would have been punting from his end zone. Mike Ditka was our special teams coach that year, and he was a wild man. Each week he told us we would be facing the best special teams in the league. Sometimes we would ask, "Didn't we see the best team last week?" And he wouldn't answer.

He had devised a new punt block especially for the Super Bowl, and now was the perfect time to run it. Instead of returning the punt, Mike had me blocking the punt. He had me on the line of scrimmage, trying to block it by bursting through the line, right up the middle. I was to line up over the guard and wait for a split second when the ball was snapped. We had the guy to my right crossing in front of me to take the blocker out, and then I was supposed to hesitate and then take off full-speed toward the theoretically open hole.

The Steelers lined up in their typical punt formation. This was a very exciting moment in the Super Bowl. There was an incredible tension in the air. I loved it. You can just imagine—the Steelers were backed up and everyone knew a punt block was coming. We had the chance for a game-changing play, and because it was against those nasty Steelers, it made it even more exciting.

Everything was set in motion when the ball was snapped back to the punter. I delayed just as planned and then blasted off as fast as I could. To my amazement, no one touched me—I broke completely free! My next stop was the punter. Usually, it never happens the way it is designed. Generally, the linemen would clog up and someone would block you, but I was free and headed right toward the punter. When he dropped the ball to punt, I quickly stretched out my arms. The ball and his foot made contact, and the ball started upward. Much to my dismay, I watched the football, as if in slow motion, breeze right between my outstretched arms, into the air and down the field.

To think, an inch or so either way and I would have blocked the ball into their end zone. We could have recovered it for a touchdown, or at the very least, the momentum, which was already in our favor, would have swung even more, and it would have been difficult for the Steelers to overcome. We could have won the game. All of our lives would have been changed. Perhaps more of our guys would have made it into the NFL Hall of Fame. In my dreams, I always block it!

CLIFF'S TALE

Mind Games Super Bowl XIII

I don't like to talk or even think about our Pittsburgh Super Bowls. Though they were closely fought battles, they bring back few, if any, good memories. The Steelers were a very good team, but I feel we could, and should, have beaten them in both of those Super Bowls. Many Dallas Cowboys did not become members of the NFL Hall of Fame because of the major influence of those games. Some Steelers made it who otherwise might not have. Our team had equally great players. Strategically, I don't feel that we used our most effective defenses against their very potent, but simple, offensive scheme. We made changes to some of our strongest defenses to counter a few of the Steelers' plays.

Terry Bradshaw was the type of QB who was not affected as much by the movement and deception of our Flex defense. He took simple keys and made quick commitments, then threw hard. Many times he would try to force the ball into double coverages with steam on his passes rather than the finesses of attacking a specific defensive weaknesses. Most times he was successful, even when he relied on the strength of his passing arm and hitting an open receiver rather than on taking keys from defenses and throwing away from their strengths. Our defensive game plan was to put Terry under pressure with some new special nickelback blitzes in passing

When Cliff blitzed, Terry Bradshaw knew the middle was open.
Photo courtesy of the Dallas Cowboys

situations, and we also redesigned some of our old standby defenses in a futile attempt to confuse him. It didn't work.

The free safety position, by definition, allowed me to help others on defense. I had the freedom to make tackles at the line of scrimmage or guard against, knock down, or intercept deep passes to receivers who had beaten our cornerbacks. One part of a safety's game is to keep the QB guessing and not be predictable. Disguise was key. I could not let the QBs know what I was doing. I was helping other positions more than individually covering specific receivers man to man, which I did sometimes in certain situations.

In the Pittsburgh Super Bowls, some of the big plays against us came when I was on a safety blitz up the middle. On one of these blitzes, Larry Cole and I got to Terry, but we were a millisecond too late. Cole caught Bradshaw right on the chin with his forearm and knocked him out of the game. It was in the fourth quarter of Super Bowl X. As I was lying on top of him, the last thing Bradshaw saw was Swann making a sensational leaping catch in the deep middle of the field for a touchdown.

When I was in Bradshaw's face, blitzing and after him up the middle of the line, the obvious weakness in the defense was the long deep middle pass where I wasn't covering. Our corners had a long day in the lonely deep middle and did not have much success taking the inside away from Swann. That day, Swann made some game-breaking catches. Because of Swann's performance, he was named MVP and ultimately elected into the Hall of Fame. He did have a big day against the weaknesses in our scheme.

Two weeks before, in the AFC championship game against Oakland, Swann had been knocked out. The great Raider strong safety, George Atkinson, hit him in the back of his head with his fist and cold-cocked him on a pass route, which resulted in a minor concussion.

By beating the Raiders, the Steelers earned the trip to face us in the Super Bowl in Miami. Both teams had two long weeks to prepare. In the first of our two weeks before Super Bowl X, "press week," all the reporters were clamoring to ask me about Swann's concussion and his danger of playing again so soon.

The hungry reporters asked me if I was going to take it easy on him. I told them only logically, "Fellows, we choose this profession of football and we realize…it is a rough sport. Swann's health is not up to me. It is up to Lynn. If he comes into my area, it is his choice, and I will not be thinking about his last week's concussion. If Lynn doesn't want to endanger his health, then he shouldn't play or at least he should not come into my area." It was a statement of fact, not a threat. Swann took it as a challenge.

In the beginning of the third quarter, the Steelers called in a route that ran Swann across the middle and Stallworth on a deep post route. This was a difficult route for me at free safety. If I chose to cover Stallworth on the deep post, Bradshaw could hit Swann on the deep in-route, which was about 25 yards deep and a big play. Because of all the pregame banter, Bradshaw knew that I really wanted to get Swann. Risking Swann's health, Terry thought for sure I would go for the in-route and the possible hit, leaving the post open for Stallworth behind me for a TD over my head. They were definitely baiting me. They hoped I would be predictable.

When the play began, I saw it develop. Stallworth took off full speed on a deep post route, and Swann ran across the middle as a decoy. Much to Bradshaw's dismay, I stayed back deep with Stallworth, leaving Swann looking open going across the middle. Bradshaw then perked up and thought Lynn was open. With his rocket arm, he loaded up and started his throwing motion. I was deep enough to make the play on the post, but the instant Bradshaw committed to Swann's in-route, I broke hard toward a collision with him. Here was my chance to live up to my prediction and knock Swann out, but instead I went not for the hit but the interception.

It was too late for Bradshaw, who was watching me all the way and saw me coming off the post route, breaking for the interception. I could see the panic in his eyes as he released the ball and tried to stop his throw. Trying to stop his throwing motion meant he did not follow through all the way on his pass, which created a strange spin on the ball similar to a knuckleball thrown by a baseball pitcher. The timing had to be perfect. I knew I had a pick and broke right in front of Swann for the ball, but just as the ball reached me it wobbled and floated just a little bit over my hands and fell to the ground, an incomplete pass instead of an interception. I couldn't believe it! I was really upset. Both Bradshaw and Swann were lucky. How did that happen?

This is one of those plays that I go over in my mind. Did I make the right decision? What if I had just laid Swann out? Who knows? Even with planning and preparation, choice, timing and luck are all factors in destiny.

CHARLIE'S TALE

Fate Rules Super Bowl XIII

Coach Landry's unemotional, analytical approach to life was hard to grasp until you got used to it. Upon reporting to Thousand Oaks, California, for training camp opening the 1979 season, Tom Landry summed up our 1978 season with a report and thus a reason for our Super Bowl XIII loss to Pittsburgh.

"We lost the game because of these three reasons," he calmly reported. He mistakenly assumed all of us were as "matter-of-fact" as he was.

"Number one: Jackie Smith's dropped touchdown pass in the end zone. Number two: Charlie Waters tackled the official rather than Franco Harris. Number three: Randy White fumbled a kickoff."

After this report, we were supposed to all put it to bed and go about our business for what was ahead in 1979. Easy for Coach Landry, but hard for us…especially those who had played a role in the "big three."

Randy White, who fumbled a kickoff, took it the hardest. He was such a dedicated teammate and the best pure football player I had ever met. He hated to lose. Being singled out to the team as one-third of the reason for losing the Super Bowl staggered the Manster. He was so sensitive.

Randy was one of the four huge linemen who made up our wedge on the kickoff return team. After a Pittsburgh touchdown late in the game, they squibbed the kickoff and it bounded directly to Randy.

He instinctively snagged the ball, tucked it away and started to advance it. The problem was that he tucked it away with his cast-covered forearm. The cast was protecting his broken wrist. When he was hit, he had no chance to hold on to the ball with that cast on. He fumbled and Pittsburgh recovered. They held the momentum and converted that short drive into a touchdown. That was the third of the loss that was credited to Randy White.

I, too, struggled with my share in the loss, but over the years I had become semi-calloused to TL's coolness; therefore I didn't take it as hard as Randy.

On third down and 12 from our 25-yard line, Pittsburgh audibled an inside dive play to Franco Harris. By running the ball, it showed they were comfortable with a field goal in that situation and didn't want to risk a turnover with the long yardage needed for a first down. Surely that simple running play was not designed to get 12 yards and a first down, much less a touchdown.

When the ball was snapped, I read the play perfectly and closed the gap from my eight-yard depth to the line of scrimmage. I never took my eyes off Franco. I was comforted to see the hole Franco was running through wasn't very wide. That reduced his options, as he had little room to cut. I was prepared to tackle Franco and hold them short of the first down.

The tackle on Franco never happened. Eyes wide open, I moved in on Franco in an attempt to make a sure tackle, only to end up grabbing an armful of the official, who had backed right into me. Where in the world did he come from? Why the umpire, who aligns himself a yard deeper and offset to one side of the linebacker, decided to "clear himself" on the side that Franco was running on, is a mystery.

The umpire is supposed to get out of the way. Cliff and I always verbally warned them early in every game about their positioning. If they continued to get in the way, sometimes we would deliver a blow with a forearm shiver to their head or drive a helmet into their back, to send a more persuasive message. They usually made it a point to know where Cliff and I were. Not in the case of Super Bowl XIII.

Jackie Smith—the agony.
***Photo by John Rhodes/*The Dallas Morning News**

From the angle of the video that we watched after the game, it was very easy to see the official, but from my angle on the field, it was impossible. No excuse, though. It was my job to make the play. Regardless, official or no official, I accepted my third of the loss.

The final third, a wide-open Jackie Smith dropping Roger Staubach's nearly perfectly thrown pass, still haunts many Dallas fans. Jackie's body writhing on the ground in the end zone after the ball had fallen harmlessly to the turf is an image burned into the memory of thousands of Dallas faithful. It is such an important moment in NFL history that it is framed and displayed at the Pro Football Hall of Fame.

On second and seven from the seven-yard line, Coach Landry called a play-action pass. The Steelers bit, just like it was drawn up. Jackie Smith, trying to sell a run, had stunned his linebackers and then released into the wide-open area that the Steelers had vacated.

Roger, in an attempt to protect Jackie, took the blame and apologized for throwing the ball so softly. Not the case. Jackie just dropped the touchdown. We could feel the defeated moans originating in Dallas all the way in Miami. We settled for a field goal, and Pittsburgh took over the momentum and never lost it.

Hall of Fame tight end Jackie Smith cried with all of us in the locker room—reason number one.

CHAPTER 7

War Stories

CHARLIE'S TALE: *Semi-Tough*

When you elect to play football, you forfeit the right to stay healthy. Injuries are just a part of the game. Some are really bad and some are not so bad, but all injuries are bad.

There is the belief that playing on artificial turf results in more injuries than playing on natural grass—more knee injuries, more shin splints, more busted bursa sacs and more strawberries.

Texas Stadium's original turf had very little padding protecting us from the concrete slab it lay on. It was quick, but it was hard.

One fall afternoon we were hosting the New England Patriots in a rare interconference battle. Halfway through the second quarter, New England had mounted a steady drive past midfield. The game was tied 7-7. Their score was the result of a Tony Dorsett fumble returned for a touchdown. Until then, they had not cracked our territory.

On third down and five, Steve Grogan dropped back and found his All-Pro tight end, Russ Francis. I had good coverage on him, but Grogan threw a perfect pass, just out of my reach. Russ caught it, and I immediately wrestled him to the ground. We spun around and crashed in a heap as I frantically tried to keep him from making the first down. When we slammed to the hard turf, I felt a sharp pain shoot up my left arm, originating in my left hand. Just as baseball players never rub a spot that was hit by a pitch, football players don't whine about not-so-bad injuries. Ignoring the pain, I rolled over, gathered myself, and trotted back to the huddle.

The Patriots were short of the first down, but they were going for it on the fourth. Nothing was said when our short-yardage defensive personnel joined us. Before getting the defensive call, I analyzed the situation; it looked like they were less than a yard short. My left hand was still kind of numb. There was a tingling feeling, like it was asleep. It didn't concern me much. It's football, after all.

When I bent over in the huddle, I rested both hands on my knees. Again, an electrical shock shot up my arm. I finally took a look at my hand. I stood up and raised my left hand and turned it so my palm was directly in front of my face.

"Aaaaugh," I yelled. "My finger's gone!"

I saw only my thumb and the next three fingers, but Cliff was quick to the rescue. "Here it is," he comforted me, as he turned my hand around to show me the little finger dangling from the joint. Damn artificial turf!

It was apparent that the ligaments were still attached—I guess that's what that white sinewy stuff was. The skin was ripped across the palm side, but skin on the back and the ligaments held the finger to my hand. There was a vacant spot where my pinky was supposed to be. The bone from my hand was exposed, and blood was gushing in rhythm with my heartbeat. I grabbed my left hand with my right, applying pressure in an attempt to slow the bleeding, and ran to the sideline.

Dr. Knight sat me on the bench and quicker than a snap he successfully manipulated the finger back into its slot. Ligaments, etc., seemed to all be in place. "Just a dislocation," he reported. Don Cochran, our trainer, sprayed it with some kind of disinfectant, placed a wad of gauze down at the joint and taped it to my ring finger.

I went back into the game, missing only one play.

At day's end, we beat New England. After the game, they sewed the finger up. When the "rip" healed, my pinky worked perfectly.

CHARLIE'S TALE

The Seasoned Vet

If you play football at any level, you are going to get hurt. I guess the big debate is differentiating between being hurt and being injured. With both comes pain. If you are injured, you usually don't play. If you are hurt, but not injured, you play. Our credo was if we got paid to play, that's what we did—we played. The only way you didn't play was if the doctor felt you might risk turning a hurt into an injury.

Most of the time the "hurts" were just that. You just hurt. If you could block it with Novocain and not risk further injury, then you "take the needle." Shots for blocking pain were like magic or a miracle. One minute you can't push off your "AstroTurf toe" and the next you can not only push off, you can run—for at least two hours. You forgot about being hurt...or injured.

Taking a shot to your hurt area in the NFL is similar to getting a shot by your dentist before he does some drilling. There are just two differences: one, the little numbing gauze they use to ease the needle entry is nonexistent; and two, the NFL shot goes directly into the exact, precise location where there is the most pain, whether the pain is from a broken big toe, bone spurs in your ankle, loose bodies in your knee or an inserted rod that was interfering with shoulder rotation—all of which I had shots for. I was, after all, a veteran.

So, that established, when our good buddy and great athlete, running back and wide receiver Mike Montgomery, had to take his first shot for pain, he called on me for advice.

On Monday before the '72 Minnesota playoff game, Mike had been experiencing some excruciating pain in his lower abdomen. On our day off he went to get it analyzed, and the diagnosis was that Mike had an advanced-stage hernia.

The doctor's recommendation was to not practice during the week to calm it down, or, if he could bear the pain, he could practice. The doctor felt that there was no way he was going to hurt it worse, it was just going to be very painful—a classic hurt, but not injured. He was a perfect candidate for a Novocain block.

He tried to practice on offensive day because Coach Landry had created much of our attack using Mike at both the running back and wide receiver positions. But Mike just couldn't go; there was just too much pain. By Friday, he was very discouraged that it wasn't improving. I counseled him to "just take the needle" on game day and testified that it was a "piece of cake." I lied.

On Saturday before the game I met privately with Coach Landry to inform him that Mike would be available through the miracle of medicine and to count him in on the attack. No reason for him to take the pain and trauma of the shot, be ready to go and then sit on the bench all day. Tom Landry needed to know. I think he appreciated me informing him, because Coach Landry loved the kind of offensive weapons Mike's versatility presented to the defense.

After the pregame warmup, in which Mike Montgomery did no more than jog around gingerly, we met in the training room. The seasoned veteran of the needle, I was going to accompany my friend through this ordeal. It was 30 minutes until kickoff, and I was "talking him down" when we entered the doctor's little X-ray room off the main training room at Texas Stadium.

Mike stripped down to his jock and lay face up on the examination table. It was just him and me in the room awaiting the doctor. I could tell he was anxious and apprehensive, so I did my best to calm him.

Finally, the doctor and his assistant arrived. He was carrying all the necessary tools on a tray. He placed the tray on the table next to Mike. He then started probing Mike's abdominal area, trying to pinpoint the most painful spot.

The most horrific knee injury we've ever seen ended versatile Mike Montgomery's football career.
Photo courtesy of Mike Montgomery

He found it as Mike yelped and grimaced. As I attempted to calm him, the doctor grabbed the syringe and held it vertically to milk a drop out, clearing the air from the needle.

I caught sight of the needle. God, it must have been 10 inches long!

Someone must have turned up the thermostat, because I felt sweat beading on my forehead. Then I witnessed the doctor take that spear and drive it into Mike's stomach three inches below his belly button. As Mike screamed, the last thing I remember thinking was, "My God, this needle is so long it's going to come out his back!"

When I awoke, I was on the floor. The doctor was hovering over me swiping smelling salts under my nose in an attempt to wake me. The "seasoned" veteran of the needle had passed out. Some help I was.

Mike was awesome that afternoon in our win. No thanks to me, he caught seven passes for more than 100 yards and gained more than 50 yards rushing, without any pain... until that night when the medicine wore off.

CHARLIE'S TALE

Windtalkers

I'd heard about it before—that uncanny, unexplained mental link family members share. I really believe Cliff and I had that same sort of connection, especially on game day.

Game plans for defense are built each week to stop the offensive trends the next opponent has established on a three- to four-game period. Down and distance, personnel, formations and game situations are the major components for setting a defensive plan.

The week of preparation for the Philadelphia Eagles was fairly predictable, as their offense was relatively simple. That simplicity made it easy for Ron Jaworski, "Jaws," to go though his progression on pass plays. They had excellent skill personnel—Pro Bowlers Harold Carmichael and Wally Henry at wide receiver, Keith Krepfle at tight end and Wilbur Montgomery at running back, all led by Jaws at the helm.

Ron was a pro's pro. He was not gifted with superb athleticism, but he made up for it with his attention to details. Reading defenses was his forte, and carrying out fakes to Montgomery set up successful play-action pass plays.

In our game plan, all formations had a set defense for that opponent during that week. The special, as Coach Landry named our automatic defense, was designed to stop the Eagles' favorite plays. Each formation had its own special, and each special had its own best change-up, just in case the special wasn't "special." Another reason for a change-up was to combat something new the Eagles might throw at us. Most offensive teams add about 30 percent new plays each week.

When the offense tricks the defense and breaks its tendencies, the defensive coaches make adjustments. These usually are implemented during a timeout or a change of possession so all players can pay attention. Because Coach Landry frowned on it, rarely did Cliff and I ever make changes on our own. Well, maybe it's better said that Coach Landry never knew when we'd make changes.

The first series against Philly, being played at the Vet, started at their own 15-yard line. Doomsday smelled blood, and we wanted to take control of the field-position game early by stopping them with a three and out.

Jaworski and company had other ideas. After two first downs, we were near midfield when the Eagles, on third and seven, came out in a slot formation (both wide receivers on the same side). It was the first slot they had showed. Our special was a three-deep zone. The corner on the two-receiver side was to harass the inside slot receiver into submission, and Cliff was to roam the middle, free.

On the opposite side, where the tight end lined up, I was responsible for forcing the end run and covering the tight end if he released and flared outside deep (which is what they did successfully the week before). The Eagles loved to sneak the tight end past the strong safety while he was busy meeting the lead blockers on the look-alike run.

The play was designed to lure the safety up by faking the run, vacating the area the tight end would settle into.

Of course that's exactly what they did. The play-action fake to Montgomery tricked our line, the linebackers, and me. But it worked on me for less than a millisecond as I read the "attitude" of the play. The integrity needed for a run was not there, so I immediately turned and jetted to a position that allowed me to cover the tight end. Our *special* was designed to take care of this play, because they had success running it last week.

Jaws came up from his play fake just in time to see me dashing back to my tight-end responsibility. He reared to throw and then had second thoughts as I entered his frame.

Ron was well trained—no panic, just progression. He stopped his motion, reloaded and calmly hit the back in the shallow flat for the first down.

Both Cliff and I had done our jobs, but we didn't make the play. Our special took care of their tendency just exactly like it was supposed to, but Jaworski's experience and poise still beat us.

I made a mental note: "At the first break in the action, change that automatic special versus a slot formation to take care of both the back and tight end." No time yet, though, as the next play was on us. They continued their drive by converting another first down. Now the ball was on our 30 and it was just the first series!

Two more semi-successful plays left the Eagles in a third and six at our 26-yard line. They broke the huddle and I saw the two receivers heading to our left together, leaving the tight end with me on the right. It was that same slot formation.

I gave the hand signal to confirm to our players that we were playing our special, knowing that Jaws knew our coverage also. We had needed to change, but there just hadn't been any time. I could not risk changing the call on the field for fear that all would not get it.

As I lined up in my force position, I turned and made direct eye contact with my buddy Cliff. We were on the same wavelength. It was strangely comforting when I focused on his expression. I winked and he acknowledged my wink with a quick nod of his head. I knew that Cliff knew what we needed to do. It was a change-up that committed me to the back in the flat and Cliff was to take the tight end, vacating the middle. It was a gamble to vacate the middle, but no guts, no glory. The rest of the team would be playing another defense, but Cliff knew and I knew, and that was all that mattered, unless, of course, they ran a completely different play.

No problem, it unfolded as planned. They didn't run a different play. Jaws faked the run to Wilbur, just like last time. The tight end released inside and headed upfield, just like last time. The back came at me as if to block, and the line fired out like a run block. All exactly like last time.

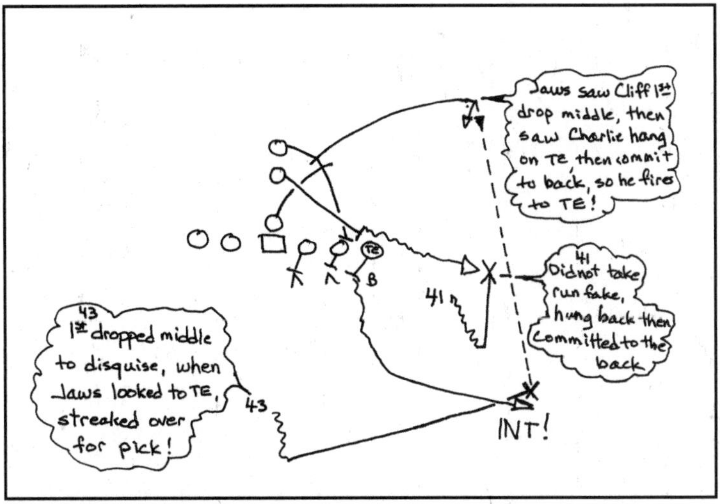

—Diagram 1—

I sniffed out the fake and hung at a spot between the tight end and the back.

When Jaws came up from his play fake, he looked right at me. He knew that I remembered the last time they had had success with that play. I tried to bait Jaworski into throwing me a pick by hanging between the receivers, but I couldn't disguise any longer when he cocked to throw. I committed to the back and suffocated the receiver, knowing that Cliff had my backside.

Ron Jaworski stutter-stepped and meticulously went through his progression. His thoughts must have been: "Cliff dropped middle…good, same zone defense, go to the tight end…no, Charlie's hanging. (See Diagram 1.)

"OK the back, fire! No, Charlie's now on him…stay calm, he can't cover both. Back to the tight end, fire."

Ron quickly turned his body to square up so that he could lob it to the tight end.

Jaworski never saw Cliff. He wasn't looking for him. Cliff wasn't supposed to be there. The pre-snap read showed Jaws a zone. The post-snap read also showed a zone. The corners were playing a zone and I was playing a zone, he thought. Cliff was supposed to be in the middle when he plays in a zone. And that's where he was...until the last second.

I didn't see Cliff either, until Ron released the ball. But like a blur out of nowhere, he streaked into the scene and slashed right in front of tight end Krepfle for a touchdown-saving interception.

Telepathy, waves, vibes, whatever—it was always hard to explain, but we had it working for us.

After a 15-yard return, Cliff and I made eye contact as we were heading off the field. We both knew the consequences if it was discovered that we risked leaving the middle wide open. So just like it was when we were on the field, we got on a parallel path again. Simultaneously we gave the other the same warning: "Don't tell Coach Landry."

CHARLIE'S TALE

Turf Battles

Cliff always looked for an angle. If you think about it, isn't that just what all professional competitors do? Most of the time, Cliff's physical style of play was his angle. Football players are, by nature, territorial. Cliff's territory, the middle of the field, was sacred ground to him. He defended it physically and with passion and prejudice. He made sure everyone was aware of the consequences if any were foolish enough to come across his territory.

He also could talk smack with the best of them. After he had delivered one of his patented hits, Cliff would offer a question to those wide receivers: "You gotta ask yourself, is it worth it to come into the middle? Seriously, is it really worth it?"

Ninety-nine percent of the pro wide receivers feared and loathed Cliff Harris. They might not know the exact time on the clock or the exact yards needed for a first down, but they always knew where he was.

Part of Cliff's philosophy was to expose the enemy's weaknesses while never revealing yours. If those wide receivers did any damage to Cliff, he never let them know. Some of those collisions that I witnessed were treacherous for the player on the receiving end, but surely they had to have been painful for him, also. But never did he outwardly admit it.

Captain Crash made an impression on every receiver he played against. Before running their routes or locating the ball, all receivers' number-one priority for survival was to locate and stay clear of Cliff, that is, if they wanted to continue playing that day. At practice, his own teammates, in an effort to always know where Crash was, awarded him a bright yellow plastic fireman's hat, complete with a red strobe light on top.

Cliff wanted to get into the psyche of all the wide receivers he competed against during his 10-year career. And he generally accomplished that, except for one man: Washington's Hall of Famer, Charley Taylor.

Charley was a physical and fearless running back-turned-wide receiver who possessed the mindset of a

After protecting his turf, Cliff would pose the question: "Was it really worth it?" ***Photo courtesy of Cowboys Weekly***

linebacker. He had long arms, great hands, ran efficient routes, had no body fat, and worst of all, he was tough! No matter how hard Cliff alone, or Cliff and I together, hit Charley Taylor, we never felt like it did any damage. He never showed it and he never let it affect his concentration. Even worse, Charley would sometimes go on the attack. Receivers just don't do that.

At RFK one wintry afternoon, it was a classic, low-scoring battle versus the evil Washington Redskins. The first five plays of Washington's first drive were running plays. Every play was a game within the game and, in this case, a war within the war. Cliff and Charley Taylor collided head on five straight times. Cliff had to first secure his run responsibility on each play before he could direct his attention to Taylor. Likewise, Taylor, from the wideout position, would execute his blocking responsibility before directing his energy to Harris.

The sixth play was a trap up the middle that Lee Roy Jordan successfully stopped. As I was closing in from the side for mop-up, I saw a blur that was Charley Taylor. He was on a mission, just like on the last five plays. I was quietly pleased his target wasn't me—it was Cliff.

Cliff, too, was revving up his jets in anticipation of the next inevitable collision. Like two dinosaurs, oblivious of the consequences that come from the effects of all-out aggression and velocity, they collided.

The result of the collision seemed like more than what their 190-pound frames could generate. The noise was deafening, and I remember thinking that with that much concentric force, something has to break, right? Wham!

Helmet to helmet, body to body, both Cliff and Charley recoiled to the ground. Cliff scrambled up first, always trying to project the most aggression, and stood over Charley as he rolled over and slowly rose to his feet. Cliff was in his face the entire time.

"That's right! Get used to it, punk. It's gonna be like that all day long!" Cliff attacked verbally, pointing his finger for emphasis. Charley quietly gathered himself and retreated to his huddle, passing me on his way. He showed no ill signs from the attack.

"All day! All day!" Cliff repeated, following Taylor, attempting to hold a position of dominance. "Get used to it!"

The instant Charley jogged across the line of scrimmage into his territory, out of our sight, Cliff fell forward into my arms, clinging desperately to keep from collapsing to the ground. He was completely limp and exhausted as he melted to his knees, managing a low-volume plea, "Please, Charlie, help. He's killing me!"

Cliff never let the enemy know.

CLIFF'S TALE

Eyes on the Ball

For me, playing in St. Louis's Busch Stadium was a cold and sterile environment, not a fun and exciting stadium. It is the same field on which the St. Louis Cardinals baseball team still plays.

The job of a free safety is to make plays from sideline to sideline. Because Busch was designed and built as a baseball field with large, flat outfield areas, it seemed to be a mile wide to me. It was difficult to tell where the sidelines were when I was standing in the middle of the field, because there was no crown. For a free safety, depth perception is critical. Cardinals quarterback Jim Hart knew that we were having trouble and took advantage of it by using speedy All-Pro wide receiver Mel Gray on up-routes along the sidelines.

It seems that every time we played the Cards in St. Louis it was a cold, bright October day. I had black painted beneath my eyes to help reduce the glare of the sun. A warmer, overcast day on a crowned AstroTurf field built just for football, with crazy fans who are close to the sidelines and bench, were perfect conditions for me. Busch was less than ideal.

The Cardinals had a potent offense lead by Hart, who later became one of my good friends. Sometimes during our games as we were lined up for play and facing each other, Jim would talk to me, even when he was at the line of scrimmage right before the ball was snapped. We tried to mess with each other's minds all day. I always tried to keep him guessing what defenses we were playing by initially running away from the areas I was to cover, then changing back to confuse him. Sometimes it worked, other times it did not. He was one of the best QBs, and he really knew how to look safeties off. He had speedy receivers who could score fast and often. He was a very smart, tactical-type QB. That, combined with an excellent touch-passing arm, made him the toughest QB I faced.

In preparation for games I spent hours watching films and analyzing formations, time, down-and-distance situations, drawing up routes and trying to understand how, when and why plays were run. I also wanted to understand why Jimmy threw passes to certain receivers at certain times. I wanted to try to figure out his personality and what made him tick. Would he take chances and try to force a ball in, or would he try to beat you by playing percentages? It was fun to try to figure out QBs like Jim. I wanted to get in his head. Knowing everything I could about him helped me anticipate, react faster and beat him.

The situation was third and eight. There were three minutes left in the fourth quarter. The Cards were leading 13-10. The ball was on the Cards' own 40-yard line on the left hash mark. The formation was a Brown left, X-spread. I knew what to expect…Fake 34, "W" post, "Y" curl and "4" shoot. That meant the halfback ran his route into the flat and the wide receiver ran a route into my area in the middle of the field.

Sure enough, the ball was snapped, and the play began to unfold in front of me. I wanted Hart to think that I was going to cover the post-route in the deep middle. When the ball was snapped, I knew that while Hart was dropping back, he was watching me to see if I was going to cover deep middle, leaving the curl-route to Gray open.

Hart only had about three seconds after the ball was snapped to make a decision: Was Gray going to be open? If so, he needed to throw the ball to him immediately. I faked a few steps to the deep middle and then quickly broke back to Gray running the curl. With Harvey Martin and Ed Jones closing in on Jim, he bit and threw the ball just where I hoped—to Gray. I laughed; I had Jimmy on this one!

As he released the ball, he saw me breaking and I'm sure he wished he had not thrown it, but it was too late. I was on the way for an interception and a touchdown because the field was wide open. My timing was perfect. The ball was heading right for my hands. The only problem was my helmet! What? My helmet?!

My helmet was a unique design at that time. It had special space-age foam padding to absorb the shock from hits. Dr. Marietta, an aerospace guy who built astronaut helmets, designed it. I had trouble with other helmets cracking during helmet-to-helmet collisions, but this one worked well.

A leather pad covered the foam in the front of my helmet that protected my frontal lobe. As I raised my head and extended my arms to catch Hart's watermelon pass, the pad squeegeed a little bit of sweat from my forehead into my eyes. Well, you can guess what happened next—everything blurred. I lost the ball. It tipped off my fingers and fell to the ground. So much for all that preparation and reading Hart's mind; now I just had to answer to Landry in our team film session.

Back in Dallas that following Monday afternoon, we were together watching the film. Sitting in the dark meeting room with the projector whirring while listening to Coach Landry critique is not a fun time. Good games or bad, it didn't matter, the environment was always tense. Landry's comment on a great play was "good play." On a bad play he would say, "You can't do things like this, Cliff," or if it was really bad, "You are playing like an amateur, not a professional."

Cliff, though best known for his big hits, was also a ball hawk.
Photo courtesy of the Dallas Cowboys

I knew my play was coming up on the reel. I knew that I could say the reason I missed the ball: "Coach, sweat was in my eyes." But, when the play came on the screen and Landry's comment was, "Cliff, you have to catch this ball," all I could reply was, "Yes, sir. I'll get it next time."

Beefcake

Like everything in life, pro football is constantly evolving. During Charlie's and my era, pro football was moving into a different phase. The thought of NFL football as a team sport with no individualism was changing. During the early years of football, stardom was the realm of the quarterback, but that also has changed. Players in all the positions are screaming, "Look at me!" Football has evolved from a purely macho team sport to an exciting form of entertainment provided by individuals playing a team sport. On Sundays, it's an alternative to going to the movies. Players capitalizing on their exposure is now commonplace.

When Charlie and I joined the team, any departure from team football was considered a distraction. Whether it was signing autographs or doing an interview with the press, it was all frowned upon by the hard-core veteran group. We were entering the era of the NFL when things began to change—drastically!

Our team and its goals were paramount to Charlie's and my personal goals. We spent countless hours running sprints, lifting weights, diagramming plays, studying computer printouts and watching films in preparation to perform our jobs perfectly for the team. We played for the love of playing and performing. Our quest for excellence was motivated by our own personal standards. We wanted to be recognized as the best in our profession. We desired that the acknowledgment came first and primarily from Coach Landry, then from our teammates and peers, and then from the rest of the world. When Coach Landry referred to us as "true professionals," we knew that we had arrived.

After some time in the league we were recognized as the best by our coaches, our teammates and our adversaries. With that notoriety came a certain freedom and independence. We began to reap the rewards. People came out to ask us for our autographs. I remember the first time that it happened to me as a Cowboy. I almost fell over. Someone wanted me to sign my name so they could keep it and take it home with them. It blew my mind.

After we played in a few Super Bowls, the autograph seekers and fans began to pick up substantially. At times it got a little out of control. People would come over to our table while we were eating out, or interrupt our conversations to ask if we would sign their napkin. We always did sign, but we also began to understand both the positives and the negatives associated with being public figures. We had very little privacy, especially in Dallas.

Charlie and I still sometimes laugh at ourselves when people scramble up to us. We think, "For heaven's sakes, folks, it's just football!" But we always appreciated the fans and genuinely felt as though we owed them our attention. Indirectly, they were paying our salaries.

There was very little fan paraphernalia available. Even the PR shots were hard to find. At the beginning of the season, a well-known Dallas sports photographer named Laughead took "publicity pictures." Laughead was a funny guy. He went to every NFL camp, so everyone's posed action shots all looked the same. There were very few alternatives to the "frozen running" pose. He would ask us to "huck and buck." That meant the following: We ran right at the camera, then just as he clicked the shutter, we turned sideways and stretched out our arms, crossing one leg over the other as if

The league's standard PR shot was the "frozen running" huck and buck pose. ***Photo courtesy of Cowboys Weekly***

fending off a blocker—and smile. If the young guys didn't know how to "huck and buck" he went through the routine himself. It was a riot! I look at some of those posed action shots today and laugh.

Exposure and money-making autograph sessions were limited. The only Dallas Cowboy paraphernalia fans could get their hands on was the real stuff discarded from the Cowboys' locker room. The explosion of the $4 billion NFL Properties had not yet begun. Those statue-like action shots were the only things players had to give to people who wanted autographs. There were no color or game-action shots to be found.

The print media that covered us worked hard to sell the product of the NFL—as hard as the NFL itself did. Fan interest sold newspapers. Interesting and clever articles were written, and rarely was there ever a negative slant. Most players were uncomfortable being interviewed and certainly did not understand the power of the press. Some of the players, though, were beginning to break out of the mold of seeing the press as an added pressure. The savvy players went from talking to them only when necessary, to seeking out reporters to write articles about them.

The new breed of young players like Butch Johnson, with his "California Quake" after touchdown receptions, tested the boundaries of team play. Moonwalks and end-zone dances were beginning to become commonplace and were not rare "hot-dog" antics.

We were beginning to find that with recognition and notoriety came some real opportunities—endorsements, autograph sessions and the best tables at restaurants. We were in the early years of what eventually became a very lucrative endorsement market.

It was during this time that Charlie realized what opportunities he had and wanted to ride that wave. He concocted what he thought was a brilliant idea toward the end of his career, and he did not clue me or anyone else in on it—he would sell a poster of himself!

During his career, all the young girls thought he was really cute and would line up for his autograph. He was a teeny-bopper favorite. He tried to parlay that popularity into a rewarding business arrangement. And so he posed for a "beefcake" poster. People went crazy over that. He sold more than 25,000 posters in a five-month period. The timing was right.

With this poster, Charlie capitalized on his popularity, but not without suffering grief from his teammates.

Poster courtesy of Kirk Bounds

Today it is commonplace to have posters of your favorite players, but the only posters available then were of the Jets' flamboyant QB Joe Namath and MLB pitcher Jim Palmer. Charlie was definitely ahead of his time, but, as you can imagine, he took a lot of flak from his buddies.

Now, moms come up to him with their teen daughters and tell Charlie that they had his poster and loved it. Some things *are* priceless!

CHAPTER 8
Big Games

CLIFF'S TALE Fast Exit

Penalties can change a game's momentum or can cause an outright loss. Successful teams always seem to get breaks from the officials. Most of the time that I was playing, the officials were either neutral or they leaned toward the Cowboys. There were those unique times, however, when things did not go our way and the officiating seemed to be biased against us.

One call that has been questioned by many people was in Super Bowl XIII against Pittsburgh. It may have cost us the game and was a good example of calls going the other way. On a safety blitz, Terry Bradshaw threw up a prayer toward Lynn Swann. Benny Barnes was the corner covering Swann, and Benny was right with him on a deep takeoff route, straight up the field near the sideline. Bradshaw threw the ball toward the middle of the field, where he knew I wasn't (I was up the middle on my blitz). When the ball was coming down, Swann tried to break inside of Benny, but he got tripped up and fell. An official by the name of Fred Swearingen threw his flag and called defensive pass interference. It was a big play for the Steelers, because up until then we had controlled the game. They got the ball on our 30-yard line. You could feel the momentum sway. It was a really poor call, and it still infuriates Dallas fans to this day. The call was so wrong that the league installed the "incidental contact" rule the next year to prevent it from happening again. It is one of those things you look back on when you lose a Super Bowl and wonder "what if?"

Most of the time, I had the favor of the back judge, who lined up behind me and was responsible for making calls like unnecessary roughness or pass interference. I would talk to them before the games and make sure that they understood I was going to play fair. I would not take cheap shots, but I was also not going to have any mercy on receivers in my area. They understood that this was football and that was the way it was to be played. Today, I would probably be fined out of the league with the new rule changes on hitting. When I played they seemed to give me a break on close calls, but I never got away with the obvious ones. It was during those gray-area times that we needed to have the officials on our side.

I did get a good break on a close call when we were playing the New York Giants in November of 1978 in Texas stadium. We were on track to win the division and go into the playoffs. Craig Morton, a former Cowboy, was their excellent quarterback. He was having a good year. Though Craig was very talented, he had lost the competition in Dallas, and

Roger Staubach took the helm at QB for the Cowboys the rest of the decade. Craig was traded to the Giants.

From his years in Dallas, Craig had a thorough understanding of the Cowboy defenses. He knew both Charlie and me from going against us every day on the Cowboys' practice field. He knew how to avoid our strengths and attack our weaknesses. He did have to figure out what defense we were playing very quickly, though, before either Cole, Harvey, Ed or Randy collapsed his pocket and took him down. A quarterback's indecision or confusion usually resulted in a sack.

The other role in my good break was played by the Giants' All-Pro tight end, Bob Tucker. He later became a good friend of mine, but at the time, he was not. He wasn't a very big guy for a tight end, but he had deceptive moves and could really catch the football. He was Craig's go-to receiver in the clutch.

The Giants were on our eight-yard line. It was at the end of the game, with less than a minute left. We were leading the Giants 9-3. They needed a touchdown to beat us. They were on the eight-yard line, and it was fourth and goal. The odds did not favor a run, so we anticipated the pass, and the call from the sidelines was a change-up-type pass defense. Defensive line coach Ernie Stautner sent in a 35 Flex Weak defense, which meant I had Bob Tucker, man to man, without help from anyone. My gut tightened. Rarely do defenders have man-to-man responsibility without any help from other DBs or LBs, except for blitzes. This was one of those rare times. This coverage was a unique call designed to confuse the quarterback and, at the same time, help the

The NFL experienced a magical year in 1977, as Craig Morton, MVP, directed the Broncos to the Super Bowl.
Photo courtesy of Cowboys Weekly

corners with double coverage on the wide receivers, so it left no one to help me. I was isolated!

Charlie would break from his strong safety position and take the inside routes away from the wide receiver on the strong side. D.D. Lewis would take the outside away from the weak-side wideout and Lee Roy Jordan would take the inside away.

The strategy was for me to cover Tucker very closely; a short pass completion meant a TD and victory for the Giants. We also needed a great rush. We wanted our D-linemen to, as Gene Stallings would say, "back thar ears" and take off. In Craig's moment of analysis, we would sack him before he could get his pass off. It was risky, but a good strategic call in this situation...if it worked. Two things had to happen: I had to cover and we had to have a great rush!

I knew Craig was watching me. Though Tucker was on the strong side, I lined up in my normal position on the weak side. My eyes were on Tucker. I did not want to give the coverage away by changing where I normally lined up. The ball was snapped. I made a quick fake move to the weak side to make Craig think I was double-covering a wideout. Then I immediately moved back to find and latch onto Tucker on the strong side. I knew from studying all our data that Bob's favorite route at the goal with Craig was a turn-in.

Sure enough, Tucker did just what I expected. I had him covered like a blanket, but at the last second he fooled me with a fake turn-in and headed towards the sideline. When he made his outside move and I realized that I was beaten, I grabbed his jersey and, as subtly as possible, yanked for a split second. I kept my elbow and arm tucked into my side so that the official standing right behind me could not see. Craig was watching me and saw that Tucker had a step on me. He was just about to throw the ball to him, when my grip stopped Tucker's move and jerked him back. That threw Craig's timing off, and he did not throw the pass. He gathered himself, and just as he was going to throw it again, my man Randy White smashed him into the turf. Craig screamed pass interference as he was falling. Tucker turned around and yelled at the official right behind me, but the zebra just shrugged.

The play took place at the end of the field, right at the entrance to the tunnel that led to the locker room. The crowd was screaming and so was Tucker! The clock clicked to zero just as the play ended. When the buzzer sounded, I took off for the exit tunnel and out of the stadium with Bob Tucker chasing me. He was right behind me yelling, "You held me, you son of a bitch!" He followed me up the tunnel and into the Cowboys' dressing room, yelling all the way. I just started laughing and he shook his head and then went over to his locker room to take his shower before the long trip home.

Sometimes winning is a function of timely breaks, or getting off the field in a hurry!

CHARLIE'S TALE

Hail Mary

One common term that has found a way into our vernacular is "Hail Mary." Whenever it is used, everyone understands just exactly what it means: On the last play, the ball is thrown as far and as high as possible and a Hail Mary prayer is said while it's in flight that a teammate will bring it down. It is a last-ditch effort against the odds—that's a Hail Mary.

In the 1975 playoff game, Dallas vs. Minnesota, we pulled off a miracle, and with it came the origin of the "Hail

Drew Pearson drove a dagger through the hearts of the Minnesota faithful by hauling in Roger's Hail Mary pass.
***Photo by John Rhodes/*The Dallas Morning News**

Mary" pass. It truly was a last-ditch effort that salvaged a win. Drew Pearson brought down the ball and answered Roger Staubach's prayers. The long, high bomb had been launched at the 50-yard line, and only our prayers kept it in the air.

The Hail Mary pass and catch put us ahead for the first time in a game that had been dominated by the Vikings. It had been a banner year for Minnesota. Fran Tarkenton set the league on fire. Their team was the top seed in the NFC and was favored to win the Super Bowl. This was to be the year Minnesota would finally shake the can't-win-the-big-one tag. Dallas, on the other hand, was lucky to be there. We snuck into the playoffs as a wild-card team.

On the last drive, our offense had the ball and was trying to pull out a win. The rest of our team was on the sidelines "believing." We knew that if a win was at all possible, Roger would find a way. He had done it so many times before, who could doubt him?

We all have our superstitious rituals to help the offense, but some were stranger than others.

Dave Edwards, our 14-year strong-side linebacker, grabbed me right after Roger took a sack on the first play of the drive and commanded, "Bucket [my roommate Walt Garrison called me Bucket because of my last name—Water Bucket], walk back here behind the bench in the direction we are going. Close your eyes and chant, 'Rabbit, rabbit, rabbit.' And do it with conviction." Dave was so serious; I didn't even bother to question this procedure. I just did it.

When Roger's pass dropped into Drew's hands, I didn't see it, as my eyes were closed. I just heard a monstrous moan and "Boos" from the stands, coupled with jubilant chaos from our bench. I grabbed my helmet and sprinted onto the field, since I was the holder on extra-point attempts. That end of the field looked like a war zone with all the debris scattered everywhere—a result of fan rebellion. Those in the end zone near the play believed that "Mr. Clutch," Drew Pearson, might have pushed off Nate Wright.

There were no flags, just cups, oranges, batteries, programs, shoes and anything else the irate fans could find.

After we kicked the extra point, we led by four with less than a minute to go in the game—all thanks to the Hail Mary. We kicked off, and the Vikings started their last chance at the 20-yard line. The first play from scrimmage, Tarkenton couldn't find a receiver and had to take a sack. So the ball was at the 10-yard line. It was second down, and our defense had just broken our huddle and waited for Minnesota to set up.

At Minnesota's Metropolitan Stadium, the end zone literally backed up to the stands. We were so close I could see the anger and frustration on the disappointed faces of the fans. They had been 40 years a bridesmaid.

I was soaking it all in when I heard a muffled clunking sound. The umpire standing right next to me suddenly fell backwards like a sack of potatoes—completely motionless. I rushed to his side and saw a huge gaping hole in his forehead, blood gushing out. I thought he had been shot! He was out cold and blood covered his face.

While the officials attended to him, I huddled with Cliff and we noticed, lying next to the fallen referee, a full fifth of Jack Daniel's Tennessee Whiskey. That whiskey bottle is thick and square, and incredibly, the glass had not busted. The official had taken the full impact of that heavy projectile, tossed from about 30 yards away.

For the first time in my life, I was afraid at a football game. Both teams were ordered to retreat to their respective bench areas while the injured official was attended to. Coach Landry instructed us that at game's end we were to "keep all armor on and sprint to the locker room."

Though Tom Landry was calm as always, there was an added dose of seriousness associated with this command.

The medics carted the official off, replaced him with the emergency official and restarted the game. Two plays later, Tarkenton's last-ditch pass fell harmlessly to the turf and ended the game.

Visions of soccer riots filled my head as I sprinted to the locker room. The Vikings fans wanted blood, and they had already gotten some!

When we entered the confines of our safe locker room under the stadium, we finally got to celebrate the miraculous victory. Roger's Hail Mary prayer had been answered. Our magic had won out again to the chagrin of the best team in the NFL that year.

Those who hated the Dallas Cowboys, especially those in that north end zone, hated us more now. Drew Pearson made the clutch catch of all clutch catches. And Roger Staubach had performed another miracle.

Sadly, Minnesota had to look to next year...yet again. That play and game left a permanent scar on those great fans of the Minnesota Vikings.

Dallas, however, smashed the Rams the next week to earn a berth in yet another Super Bowl, thanks to Drew Pearson, Roger Staubach, some sideline voodoo and a Hail Mary prayer.

CHARLIE'S TALE

The Catch

The Dallas Cowboys created a monster at the NFC championship game in January 1982 when we allowed Joe

Montana and the San Francisco 49ers to make a dramatic last-minute comeback to beat us, to represent the National Conference in Super Bowl XVI. Of course, the 49ers did have something to do with it...okay, they had a *lot* to do with it.

Not that he cared, but Joe Montana's first big-time come-from-behind victory was at my expense. That championship game was my last game as an NFL player. And it didn't end quite the way I had planned. You see, we were supposed to win that day and I was to go on to a record sixth Super Bowl, have my best game and then retire as the Super Bowl MVP.

You've got to have a dream, right?

But I should have known it wasn't going to work out that way. The first sign was when D.D. Lewis and I arrived at the players' parking lot at Candlestick Park in our limousine, four hours before the game, only to see the 49ers' veteran middle linebacker, Jack "Hacksaw" Reynolds exiting a taxi in full game uniform! Hacksaw was ready. The private parking lot for the players and the team buses was usually empty when D.D. and I arrived, but not this day. Reynolds was hunching over to clear the doorsill of the taxi. It was hard to maneuver with all that armor on—ankles and hands taped, football cleats laced up, knee, thigh and hip pads, oversized shoulder pads, neck roll brace and helmet...chin strap buckled. All of this was four hours before kickoff. He even had his eye-black smudged under his eyes.

Stepping out of the taxi, Jack's steel cleats slipped on the concrete parking lot. He stumbled to regain his balance. When he did, he and I made eye contact. What a contrast:

his game uniform versus my business suit. He growled, "Yeah! Bring it on!" I glanced over at D.D. and confirmed the obvious, "This guy is ready."

Candlestick Park is a bad place to play. It's a converted baseball stadium, the wind is always blowing unpredictably and the natural turf is a mush. The stadium is below sea level, so the rains of San Francisco never get a chance to drain away. The worn-out sod is a quagmire at season's end. The NFL gave up on emergency re-sodding and elected to spread tons of small clay pellets over the field in an attempt to soak up the moisture. The field was then spray-painted green, complete with yard lines so it looked perfect for TV...before the game anyway.

The game that followed was opposite of the field conditions. It was a great game—one of the classics. Hacksaw Reynolds, the entire 49ers team and especially Joe Montana *were* ready.

I'm convinced that if my partner Cliff had still been playing, it would have been a different outcome.

San Francisco and Dallas battled back and forth. With four minutes left in the game, the Cowboys held a four-point lead. The Niners started their last drive on their own 11-yard line. Super Bowl XXVI, here we come. Nobody could drive the ball 89 yards against the Doomsday II defense—nobody, of course, except Joe Montana.

And that's exactly what he did. Dink passes here, scramble there, end runs and quick traps, and before I knew it, the 49ers were at our seven-yard line with less than a minute to go. It was now third down and goal. We all knew they had to throw into the end zone, as a field goal couldn't win the game.

"We can stop them!" I reassured my teammates in the huddle, as I called a defense that doubled-teamed Joe Montana's favorite receiver, Dwight Clark.

"Set! Hut!" Montana took the snap and dropped back. He was pressured immediately and drifted out of the pocket to his right. I was four yards deep in the end zone blanketing my tight end, but also allowing myself to witness history.

Under heavy siege, Montana slung a desperation effort over the outstretched hands of a pursuing D.D. Lewis and Ed "Too Tall" Jones. The ball drifted to the back of the end zone and I calculated the trajectory. Surely this "duck" would fall incomplete, far past the back line of the end zone. But just as I had that thought, Clark, looking as though he had bounced off a trampoline, leaped into the air, hung there and not only did he catch the pass, he somehow managed to come down with his feet inside the line. Touchdown! "The Catch."

It was over.

My dream finish was ruined.

I crumbled to my knees. The mushy clay gave a little as I sank, and then, recognizing the weight of the moment, I dramatically fell forward and lay face first in the end zone. The deafening roar of the 49ers' faithful blasted through my head.

When my facemask hit the ground, it provided no protection from the mush. I managed to push myself back up to my knees and had the presence of mind to capture both the gravity and irony of the moment.

Appealing to the higher power, I begged, "Where is Cliff when I really need him?" ***Photo courtesy of the Dallas Cowboys***

"Well...perfect," I sarcastically reported to myself. "Instead of MVP of the Super Bowl, here I am ending my career with my face buried in green kitty litter!"

Editor's Note

Charlie Waters didn't get the dream finish he had hoped for with the Dallas Cowboys.

Waters was on the field with the rest of the Cowboys defense in the final minute of the NFC Championship Game on January 10, 1982, when San Francisco receiver Dwight Clark made what will forever be known as "The Catch."

Clark's leaping grab in the back of the end zone for a 6-yard touchdown pass from backpedaling quarterback Joe Montana capped an 89-yard drive for a 28-27 victory that sent the 49ers to the Super Bowl.

Instead of a chance to end his career by holding up a third Super Bowl championship trophy and maybe being the MVP of his final game, Waters had his face buried in the muddy, pellet-covered turf at Candlestick Park in a crushing loss.

As agonizingly close as Waters and Dallas came to the Super Bowl in the safety's final career game—after also losing in the NFC Championship Game at Philadelphia the previous season—it would still be more than a decade after that before the Cowboys finally made it to another Super Bowl.

Harris and Waters were both rookies during the 1970 season when the Cowboys played in their first Super Bowl—a 16-13 loss to the Baltimore Colts in Miami.

The safeties got to be part of Dallas' first five Super Bowl appearances, all in a span of nine seasons (1970-78). That included championship seasons in 1971 and 1977 when the Cowboys won two Super Bowls played in New Orleans (24-3 over Miami, then 27-10 over Denver).

After Waters played his final game, two years after Harris and quarterback Roger Staubach had finished their playing careers, there would be some significant changes and some unexpected low moments for the Cowboys before they would get back to the top.

Tom Landry's Final Seasons

Tom Landry was the first coach for the Dallas Cowboys and became an iconic figure on the sideline. He wore that trademark fedora. He peered forward with those steely eyes. His arms were most often folded in front of him with a playsheet in his hand. And he rarely—at least outwardly—showed any change of emotion no matter what was happening on the field.

Landry was hired even before the NFL had approved the new expansion team in Dallas and before it was known as the Cowboys. They started with a winless inaugural season (0-11-1 in 1960) that was part of five consecutive losing seasons to begin their history.

Then they became consistent winners and earned the moniker of "America's Team."

After making the playoffs for the first time in 1966, the Cowboys missed the postseason only twice over 20 seasons.

The Cowboys lost their third consecutive NFC Championship Game in January 1983, at Washington. They never won another playoff game under Landry. Dallas lost in the first round of the playoffs to the Los Angeles Rams to end the 1983 and 1985 seasons.

Dallas slipped to a losing record for the first time since 1964 when they ended the 1986 season with a five-game losing streak for a 7-9 record. They were 7-8 a year later and then 3-13 in 1988 in what would mark the end of Landry's 29-season stint as the Cowboys coach.

Landry coached 418 regular-season games for Dallas. Only George Halas and Don Shula coached more NFL games. Halas and Shula are also the only coaches with more than Landry's 250 wins.

Jerry Jones Buys the Cowboys

In February 1989, Arkansas oil man Jerry Jones bought the Cowboys and Texas Stadium from Bum Bright for $140 million. When Jones bought the team, the co-captain of the University of Arkansas' 1964 national championship team brought with him one of his former teammates as the new Dallas coach—Jimmy Johnson.

Tom Landry cleaned out his office at the team's Valley Ranch facility two days after Jones bought the team.

The first draft pick by Jones came two months later when the Cowboys used the No. 1 overall selection to get quarterback Troy Aikman.

One of the biggest game-changers for the rebuilding Cowboys came on October 12, 1989, when running back Herschel Walker was traded to Minnesota for five players, five conditional draft picks and a first-round pick in the 1990 draft. Among the players Dallas actually got because of that trade were NFL career rushing leader Emmitt Smith and safety Darren Woodson, the team's career tackles leader.

Smith was drafted 17th overall in 1990. Woodson was the 37th overall pick in 1992, the fourth selection by the Cowboys leading into a season that would also become the start of an incredible run.

The Triplets and Three Titles

Troy Aikman, Emmitt Smith and Michael Irvin became known as "The Triplets" and helped return the Cowboys to their championship ways.

Irvin was a first-round pick in 1988, drafted by the Cowboys before Tom Landry's final season. Irvin was a big receiver who played at the University of Miami for Jimmy Johnson, who a year later replaced Landry as the Cowboys coach after Jerry Jones bought the team.

Like Landry in his first year as coach, Aikman was winless and lost 11 games in his first season as the Cowboys quarterback. Aikman lost all 11 of his starts as a rookie in 1989 when the Cowboys were 1-15 (Steve Walsh was the starter in the victory at Washington).

Smith was drafted by the Cowboys as the 17th overall pick in 1990, when they went 7-9.

Dallas finally made the playoffs again for the first time in six seasons in 1991. The Cowboys had a successful postseason return with a 17-13 victory at Chicago in an NFC Wild Card game. They lost at Detroit the following week in the divisional playoffs, but were poised for what was then an unprecedented championship stretch.

Led by the Triplets, the Cowboys went 13-3 in 1992 and made it to their first Super Bowl in 14 seasons. They won the NFC Championship Game at San Francisco 30-20 in what was their first playoff game against the 49ers since "The Catch" by Dwight Clark 11 years earlier. Dallas then crushed Buffalo 52-17 in Super Bowl XXVII in Pasadena, Calif.

Dallas followed a similar path the following season, beating San Francisco in another NFC Championship Game—this one 38-21 at Texas Stadium. The Cowboys then again decisively defeated Buffalo in another Super Bowl (30-13 in Atlanta) to give them their first back-to-back Super Bowl championships.

Jimmy Johnson left the Cowboys after those back-to-back Super Bowl championships and was replaced by Barry Switzer.

Even though the 49ers beat Dallas 38-28 in the NFC Championship Game at the end of the 1994 season, preventing the Cowboys from having the chance to be the first team to win three consecutive Super Bowls, they rebounded the next season with a championship first.

Flamboyant cornerback Deion Sanders arrived in Dallas in 1995 after being part of that San Francisco team that won the Super Bowl the previous season.

(Sanders was among the class inducted into the Pro Football Hall of Fame in August 2011. Aikman, Smith, and Irvin were already members of that exclusive group.)

With "Prime Time" joining the Triplets, even though Sanders didn't sign with Dallas until the second week of the season and was sidelined until halfway through the season because of injury, the Cowboys were on their way to another Super Bowl. They beat Philadelphia and Green Bay in the NFC playoffs before a 27-17 win over the Pittsburgh Steelers, an old nemesis.

Cliff Harris and Charlie Waters were part of two NFC championship teams in Dallas that suffered close Super Bowl losses to Pittsburgh—at the end of the 1975 season (21-17) and the 1978 season (35-31).

The championship over the Steelers made Dallas the first team to win three Super Bowls in a four-year span. That feat was later matched by the New England Patriots, who were Super Bowl champions in the 2001, 2003 and 2004 seasons.

Super Bowl XXX against the Steelers was also the Cowboys' record eighth Super Bowl appearance.

That wasn't equaled until February 2011, when the Steelers played in their eighth Super Bowl. That came in the Steelers' 31-25 loss to Green Bay at Cowboys Stadium, the shiny $1.2 billion facility that America's Team had moved into in 2009.

At least the Steelers didn't get to play a Super Bowl at Texas Stadium, the once modern facility with the hole in the roof that Harris and Waters called home for most of their careers. Texas Stadium opened midway through the 1971 season, the second in the league for the two safeties. That was also the season the Cowboys won their first Super Bowl championship.

Cliff and the Ring of Honor

Going into the 2011 season, it had been six years since anyone had been put into the Dallas Cowboys prestigious Ring of Honor—a tradition that began in 1975 with the induction of defensive tackle Bob Lilly, who was nicknamed "Mr. Cowboy" after he was the team's first-ever draft pick in 1961 out of nearby TCU and became a star on defense.

The last Ring of Honor induction ceremony was during a Monday night game in 2005 when the Triplets—Troy Aikman, Emmitt Smith, and Michael Irvin—were honored together. All are also in the Pro Football Hall of Fame.

That came a year after Cliff Harris and offensive lineman Rayfield Wright (1967-79) were inducted, their names added to the Ring of Honor around Texas Stadium. At the time, they joined only 10 other players along with former team president/general manager Tex Schramm and former coach Tom Landry.

After the Cowboys lost to the Baltimore Ravens in their final game at Texas Stadium on December 20, 2008, which was 16 months before the stadium in Irving with the hole in the roof was imploded, the Ring of Honor was incorporated as part of the new Cowboys Stadium in Arlington that opened before the 2009 season.

Quarterback Roger Staubach was the sixth player in the Ring of Honor. His induction in 1983 was the last until Jerry Jones bought the team in 1989.

Linebacker Lee Roy Jordan was inducted in October 1989, four years before Landry was put in the Ring of Honor. While all the players had their jersey number and names etched on the stadium façade, the entry for Landry includes an image of his famed fedora.

Harris was a six-time Pro Bowl safety and appeared in 21 playoff games (five Super Bowls) wearing No. 43 for the Cowboys.

Harris was teammates at some point with nine Ring of Honor members: running back Tony Dorsett, wide receiver Bob Hayes, linebacker Chuck Howley, Jordan, Lilly, defensive back Mel Renfro, Staubach, defensive tackle Randy White, and Wright.

Of that group, seven are also in the Pro Football Hall of Fame—Dorsett, Hayes, Lilly, Renfro, Staubach, White, and Wright. Harris and Jordan were finalists for the Pro Football Hall—Jordan in 1988 and Harris in 2004.

Thanksgiving Day Wonders

Clint Longley isn't the only backup quarterback in Dallas Cowboys history whose biggest game with a star on his helmet came during a comeback victory on Thanksgiving Day, the holiday synonymous with the Cowboys having a home game.

Several years before Jason Garrett became the Cowboys' offensive coordinator in 2007, and then added the title of head coach midway through the 2010 season, he spent seven seasons (1993-99) as Troy Aikman's backup. Playing behind the eventual Hall of Fame quarterback who won three Super Bowl championships, Garrett appeared in only 23 games with just nine starts for the Cowboys.

One of Garrett's starts came on Thanksgiving Day 1994, when the third-stringer was needed against Green Bay because the Cowboys were without Aikman and Rodney Peete.

Dallas trailed 17-6 at halftime before scoring 36 second-half points in a 42-31 victory over Brett Favre and the Packers. Garrett finished 15-of-26 passing for 311 yards and two touchdowns, his best game under center for Dallas.

That came 20 years after Longley had his memorable Thanksgiving Day at Texas Stadium against the rival Washington Redskins. Roger Staubach got knocked out of the game in the second half, and Dallas trailed 16-3 when Longley made his first-ever appearance for the Cowboys.

(Charlie Waters tells tales about that game, Longley's pony and the quarterback's training camp confrontation with Staubach in an earlier section of this book.)

Longley completed 11 of 20 passes for 203 yards and two touchdowns against the Redskins. He threw a 35-yard touchdown to Billy Joe DuPree and then a game-winning 50-yard TD pass to Drew Pearson in the final minute for a 24-23 Cowboys victory.

A Lot of Long Offseasons

The season after their third Super Bowl title in four years, the Cowboys won their 1996 NFC Wild Card game, 40-15 over Minnesota.

What followed was a loss at Carolina in the NFC Division playoff the next weekend, starting what would become the longest drought in team history between postseason victories.

The Cowboys lost NFC Wild Card games in 1998 and 1999—to Arizona and then at Minnesota—in their only two seasons under Chan Gailey, already the team's third head coach since the end of Tom Landry's tenure.

Dave Campo, who later returned to the Cowboys staff and in 2011 marked his fourth season back as their secondary coach, was the head coach for three consecutive 5-11 seasons (2000-02).

After Campo's time as head coach in Dallas, owner Jerry Jones convinced two-time Super Bowl champion coach Bill Parcells to return to the sideline with the challenge of restoring the winning edge to America's Team. It was the second time Parcells coached again after saying he was retired. He was an NFL analyst for ESPN when Jones hired him, and in the 2011 season was back on air with the cable network after more than three seasons in a non-coaching role in the Miami Dolphins organization.

Parcells took over in 2003, and the Cowboys immediately responded with a 10-6 regular season to get back to the playoffs. They lost 29-10 at Carolina in an NFC Wild Card game.

Later came two near-misses in the playoffs after undrafted free agent Tony Romo took over at quarterback. Romo's first playoff loss was in Parcells' final game before he again retired from coaching.

In their 2006 NFC Wild Card game, Parcells' last game, Romo botched the hold of a late chip-shot field goal that would have put Dallas ahead at Seattle. Romo picked up the ball and tried to scramble to the end zone, but was tackled short of the goal line while trying to convert the messed-up play into a touchdown. In the locker room after the 21-20 loss, Romo—who had become a Pro Bowl pick that season even though he wasn't a starter until the seventh game—tearfully apologized to teammates.

Wade Phillips took over as coach in 2007. The Cowboys went 13-3 in the regular season to win their first NFC East title since 1998. The Cowboys had a first-round bye and home-field advantage in the playoffs. But they lost 21-17 to the New York Giants, the division rival they had defeated twice that regular season.

Romo had a fourth-down pass intercepted in the end zone by the Giants with nine seconds left. After that playoff loss, receiver Terrell Owens' lips quivered and he became teary during his postgame interview while defending the young quarterback who had another Pro Bowl season end with a gut-wrenching play.

It wasn't until 2009, the first season in the sparkling new $1.2 billion Cowboys Stadium, that Dallas finally won another playoff game. After ending the regular season with consecutive shutout victories for the first time in franchise history, including 24-0 over Philadelphia in the finale, they beat the Eagles at home again (34-14) the following week in an NFC Wild Card game.

That was the first playoff victory in 13 seasons, ending the longest postseason drought in team history, though Dallas was still looking for its ninth Super Bowl appearance and sixth championship.

Jerry Jones went into the 2010 season with dreams of his Cowboys being the first team in NFL history to play a Super Bowl in their own home stadium. Instead, Dallas lost seven of its first eight games. Phillips, the head coach and defensive coordinator, was fired. Offensive coordinator Jason Garrett, a former Cowboys backup quarterback behind Troy Aikman, was named interim head coach.

The interim tag was removed after the season and Garrett in 2011. He was the Cowboys' seventh head coach in 23 seasons after Tom Landry had roamed the Dallas sideline for the franchise's first 29 seasons.